## DATE DUE

| | | | |
|---|---|---|---|
| | | | |
| | | | |
| | | | |
| | | | |
| | | | |
| | | | |
| | | | |
| | | | |
| | | | |
| | | | |
| | | | |
| | | | |
| | | | |
| | | | |
| | | | |
| | | | |
| | | | |
| | | | |

DEMCO 38-296

# ELECTRONIC INFORMATION DISTRIBUTION IN TOURISM AND HOSPITALITY

# Electronic Information Distribution in Tourism and Hospitality

## P. O'CONNOR

*Institut de Management Hôtelier International*
*Groupe ESSEC, Cergy-Pontoise, France*

n of CAB INTERNATIONAL

CABI *Publishing*
CAB INTERNATIONAL
Wallingford
Oxon OX10 8DE
UK

Tel: +44 (0)1491 832111
Fax: +44 (0)1491 833508
Email: cabi@cabi.org

CABI *Publishing*
10 E. 40th Street
Suite 3203
New York, NY 10016
USA

Tel: +1 212 481 7018
Fax: +1 212 686 7993
Email: cabi-nao@cabi.org

A catalogue record for this book is available from the British Library, London, UK.

**Library of Congress Cataloging-in-Publication Data**

O'Connor, Peter.
  Electronic distribution technology in the tourism and hospitality
industries / P. O'Connor.
     p.    cm.
  Includes bibliographical references and index.
  ISBN 0-85199-283-8 (alk. paper)
   1. Hospitality industry--Data processing.   2. Tourist trade-
-Information services.   3. Computer network resources.   4. Internet
(Computer network) (.    I. Title.
  TX911.3.E402797   1999
  647.94'0285--dc21                                    98-33432
                                                          CIP

ISBN 0 85199 283 8

The content of this textbook is intended to provide a general background guide to the subject matter. All information is believed to be correct at the time of publication. Specialist advisors should be consulted before taking any action based on the information contained in this report.

Typeset by Wyvern 21 Ltd, Bristol
Printed and bound in the UK by Biddles Ltd, Guildford and King's Lynn

# Contents

# List of Tables

# List of Figures

# Acknowledgements

Many people have, directly and indirectly, contributed to this book. It represents the first comprehensive synthesis of the information available on electronic distribution and its effect on the tourism and hospitality sectors. Its strength is that it brings together the ideas, concepts and philosophies of a great many people, and integrates them into a comprehensive whole.

This text is the culmination of nearly 2 years of work, and is the product of the study of hundreds, if not thousands, of articles, scores of presentations and countless interviews and conversations. To thank everyone who has made a contribution would be impossible. However, the following people have made a significant impact on the thinking behind this text, and I would like to express my sincere gratitude to them for their contributions:

Victor Brophy of eCommerce Ireland
Frederique Battut of Degriftour
Dimitrios Buhalis of the University of Westminster
Philipe Dealaquis of The Hotel Guide (THG)
Andrew Frew of Napier University
Karsten Karcher of Imminus
Carl Marcussen of the Research Centre of Bornholm, Denmark
Dick Moore of the Cornell School of Hotel Administration
John Rafferty of Bord Failte – the Irish Tourist Board
Patrick Savourey of Groupe Accor.

I would also like to acknowledge the help and assistance of Tim Hardwick and Ali West at CABI *Publishing*, who could not have been more accommodating. Lastly, I'd like to thank my colleagues here at Institut de Management Hôtelier International (IMHI), in particular Gerard Guibilato, Micheal Nowlis and Sandra Richez for their support for the project.

# Abbreviations

| | |
|---|---|
| ACP | airline control protocol |
| CD | compact disk |
| CRO | central reservation office |
| CRS | central reservation system |
| DICIRMS | destination integrated computer information reservation management systems |
| DMS | destination management system |
| EBIT | earnings before interest and tax |
| GDS | global distribution systems |
| HIRO | Holiday Inn Revenue Optimizer |
| IPO | initial public offering |
| IT | information technology |
| OAG | *Official Airline Guide* |
| PC | personal computer |
| PMS | property management system |
| RTO | regional tourism organization |
| SME | small and medium-sized enterprises |
| THISCo | The Hotel Industry Switching Company |
| TIC | tourist information centre |
| TIS | Tyrol Information System GmbH |
| WTO | World Tourism Organization |

# Introduction: the Importance of Information

A traveller without knowledge is a bird without wings.

(Sa'Di Gulistan, 1258, quoted by Kotler in 1984)

Tourism is reputed to be the world's largest industry. Its revenues support a significant proportion of the economies of many nations and it is one of the largest employers worldwide. Its contribution to gross national product, employment and regional development are well documented and, unlike many other sectors, it is forecast to grow in importance in the coming decades as leisure time increases.

Tourism is acknowledged to be very information intensive – in fact, information has been described as the 'lifeblood' of the industry, as without it the sector could not function (Sheldon, 1993a). Tourists need information before going on a trip to help them plan and choose between options, and also increasingly need information during the trip as the trend towards more independent travel increases. This demand for information also reflects a more subtle issue: the annual holiday or even the weekend break is increasingly associated with enormous financial and emotional risk. In Western society in particular, time has become a scarce commodity and, particularly for couples, synchronically shared time is even more elusive. Therefore, for many consumers their annual holiday represents a major emotional investment that cannot easily be replaced if something goes wrong (Pollock, 1995a). Therefore, since travellers cannot pre-test the product or easily get their money back if the trip does not meet up to their expectations, access to accurate, reliable, timely and relevant information is essential to help them make an appropriate choice. As Buhalis (1997) points out 'the greater the degree of perceived risk in a pre-purchase context, the greater the consumer propensity to seek information about the product'.

This need for information is heightened by certain characteristics of the tourism product. Foremost among these is its intangibility –

unlike manufactured goods, the tourism product cannot be inspected prior to purchase and therefore it is almost completely dependent on representations and descriptions to help consumers make a purchase decision (Go and Pine, 1995). It is also fixed geographically, and thus the customer must travel – and thus in effect consume the product – in order to experience what they are buying (Bennett, 1993). Two other characteristics are its complexity and its interdependence. Individual tourism products are diverse, and in many cases it is this heterogeneity which makes them attractive in the first place. In addition, tourism products are rarely bought individually, and 'the endless combinations and permutations of alternative travel routes, transportation modes, time and lodging accommodation make travel decisions difficult even for the initiated' (Kaven, 1974). Suppliers, therefore, face a challenge, which Kaven has poetically described as trying 'to gain identity with untold millions of potential customers covering the whole spectrum of incomes, interests, knowledge, sophistication and needs'. Even the simplest trip means trying to match the expectations of diverse travellers to the bewildering array of choices and options provided by millions of tourism suppliers, each trying to differentiate themselves from their competitors. Given that millions of people travel every day, it can be seen that the communication of accurate, current and relevant information is essential to the efficient operation of the tourism industry.

Travellers can acquire information from a wide variety of sources, including directly from the tourism supplier. However (perhaps because of the time pressure mentioned earlier), many choose to use the services of an intermediary. These take different forms (Fig. I.1). The *travel agent* acts as both a 'search-and-book' service and as an advisor for the customer, relieving them of much of the burden of searching for suitable products, and also using their knowledge and experience to help match customers with travel experiences. *Tour operators* act as consolidators, packaging different travel components together and marketing them as a single seamless product. Some *government tourism organizations* also act as intermediaries, distributing information and brochures for tourism suppliers in their region. The primary role of each of these intermediaries is to facilitate the purchasing process, and information exchange is key to this function (Pollock, 1995a). As such, tourism suppliers must provide each one of these intermediaries with information in an appropriate format to assist them in the sales process.

Tourism suppliers have traditionally provided this information in the form of print-based media such as brochures or flyers, and through listings published in local or regional guides. However, developing and distributing such promotional material is costly, time-consuming and labour-intensive. In addition, such information is static, while

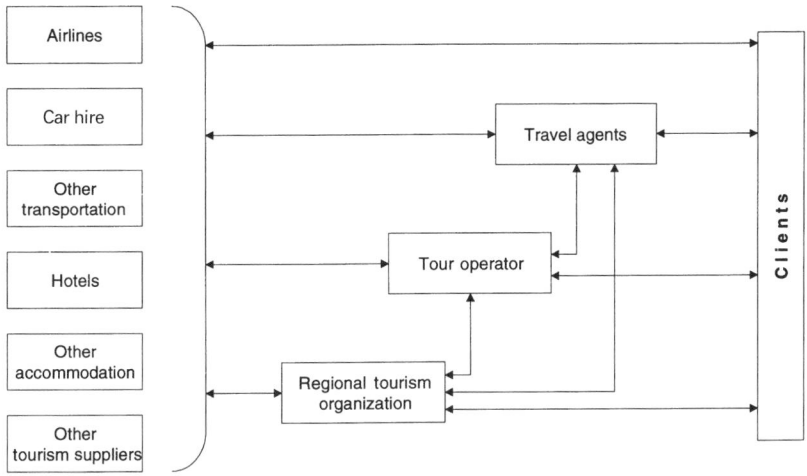

**Fig. 1.1.** Distribution channels in tourism.

much of the data needed to make a booking (such as, for example, availability and rates) changes frequently, particularly as the reservation date approaches. As a result, consumers usually have to contact the supplier directly to ensure that the product is available and to confirm the rate at which it will be sold (Bennett, 1996). Again, access to timely and accurate information is important at this stage. Tourism products are volatile in that if they are not sold, they represent lost revenue. Therefore, as their 'use by date' approaches, information about them tends to change frequently as suppliers manipulate their price in an attempt to ensure that they are all sold (Middleton, 1994). Current rates must therefore be made available to both intermediaries and direct buyers. Information also has to be able to flow in the opposite direction as, in order to make a booking, the customer's contact and payment details have to be communicated to the appropriate tourism suppliers, and thus an effective and efficient method of communication is needed (Frew and Pringle, 1995).

## 1.1 The Role of Information Technology

As can be seen from the above discussion, the exchange of information is very important at every stage in the sales cycle of the tourism product (Pollock, 1995a). Information must be able to flow quickly and accurately between the client, intermediaries and each of the tourism suppliers involved in servicing the client's needs. As a result, information technology (IT) – the amalgamation of computing, communications and electronics – has become an almost universal feature of the tourism industry (Bennett, 1993). Its power allows information to be managed more effectively, and transported worldwide almost instantly (Frew and Pringle, 1995). As a result, it has had (and continues to have) a major effect on the methods of operation of the tourism industry. However, it has not affected all functions and sectors equally. As Poon (1993) points out, it is having the greatest impact on the marketing and distribution functions, while leaving others which need more human contact relatively untouched. Similarly certain sectors, such as the airlines, have been keen adopters of technology, using it to help to manage and streamline their operations and to gain strategic advantage (McGuffie, 1994). Others, in particular the hotel sector, have been less enthusiastic, but are gradually waking up to the benefits which electronic distribution can bring. However, given the way in which IT is reshaping the basic structure of both commerce and society in general, and consumers' increased demand for information, its importance to the success of a tourism enterprise can only grow in the future (Davis and Davidson, 1991). As a result, tourism enterprises need to understand, incorporate and utilize IT strategically in order to serve their target markets, improve their efficiency, maximize profitability, enhance services and maintain long-term profitability (Bahalis, 1998).

## 1.2 Electronic Distribution

> A profession, no less than a craft, is shaped by its tools. The profession of marketing, its theories, its practices, and even the basic sciences that it draws on are determined by the tools at its disposal at any moment. When the tools change, the discipline adjusts, sometimes quite profoundly and usually quite belatedly. The introduction of television advertising 50 years ago was just such a disruptive event and marketing theory and practice are still responding, evolving their understanding of how the tool works and how its effects should be measured.
>
> (Deighton, 1996)

The points made by Deighton in a discussion on interactive marketing are especially relevant to the tourism sector, where one of its most powerful marketing tools – electronic distribution – is rapidly developing. Although traditionally not renowned for its prompt embrace of technology, electronic marketing and product distribution are quickly gaining acceptance in tourism. As a result, marketers working in the tourism sector need to be aware of this evolution and help to drive it if this trend is to realize its full potential. However, the speed of development of new distribution channels and the lack of a comprehensive source of information about the features of these systems means that the tourism industry is currently in a reactive rather than a proactive position.

This text helps to alleviate this problem by undertaking a comprehensive examination of the ways in which IT is being applied to marketing and distribution in the tourism industry. It examines how technology has been used in the past to help highlight many of the problems and limitations associated with electronically distributing the tourism product. Many initiatives currently in progress are discussed, in order to focus attention on the efforts of the industry to overcome these limitations, and the author also speculates on some of the technologies which may be used to distribute tourism products in the future. Interest in this topic appears to be high, and is being heightened by both its increasing importance and its increasing complexity. As a result, this text is aimed at a general audience and is focused on the needs and interests of managers rather than more technical computer professionals. As such, it should be of interest to managers in a wide variety of tourism enterprises (including airlines, hotels and other forms of accommodation, tourist attractions, etc.), as well as officials in government tourist offices and students of tourism management.

The text is structured into five chapters, each addressing a major topic in the evolution of tourism electronic distribution. Each chapter is followed by a series of case studies, which illustrate the experiences of real tourism enterprises with electronic distribution. The first chapter focuses on the airline sector, and documents the development of the first computerized reservation systems (CRSs), which subsequently evolved into global distribution systems (GDS) and represented the first steps along the road on which we find ourselves today. Chapter 2 focuses on the hotel sector's attempt to take advantage of electronic distribution, and examines both the evolution of their systems and current developments such as third-party reservation services and switching companies. Chapter 3 examines the problems of small and medium-sized tourism enterprises, and traces their attempts to make themselves available in the global electronic marketplace. Chapter 4 focuses on the continually growing power of the Internet and how it is redefining, amalgamating and even eliminating many of the channels that have gone before it. The final chapter looks to the future and attempts to speculate on the technologies which will have an effect on tourism distribution in the next decade.

As with any work of research, the potential exists for mistakes. This text represents the end product of the review of thousands of articles, several hundred books and scores of interviews, conversations and discussions. Obviously, given the fact that electronic media are evolving so rapidly, there is a danger that some of this material will be out of date even before it is published. The author has tried to avoid this scenario by concentrating on general trends and principles. The text does not attempt to provide a state-of-the-art assessment of the field, but rather seeks to deal with indicative trends from which important lessons can be learned or which could represent the path of the future. Any errors or omissions remain the responsibility of the author.

## I.3 About the Case Studies

Within the text, each chapter is followed by case studies relating to topics discussed in the text. In most cases, these focus on examples of tourism companies who have been pioneers in the development and application of electronic distribution, and describe developments in, or the situation in, that company at a particular point in time. The system/companies discussed include those shown in Table I.1.

These case studies are included for illustration only. They represent the position in their respective companies at a particular point in time, and are intended to stimulate thought and discussion rather than represent the current situation. Obviously, the situation will have changed since the case study was written; however, the reader should concentrate on the situation as presented, and not worry unduly about more recent developments. To get maximum benefit, the reader should try to answer some of the following questions: What should the company do next? How should they respond to the challenges that they are currently facing? Should they continue along their current course, or should they change direction? Are there any current developments in the field of electronic distribution from which they could benefit and of which they should take advantage?

Readers will learn more by analysing the situation and developing their own strategy, and subsequently discussing it with colleagues than they could by blindly following the path subsequently taken by the company under consideration.

**Table I.1.** Tourism companies discussed in the text.

| Name | Main theme of case |
| --- | --- |
| SABRE | GDS facing challenges because of its legacy database architecture and increasing competition |
| Holiday Inn | Hotel central reservation system for a centralized US hotel chain offering state-of-the-art connectivity |
| Groupe Accor | Hotel central reservation system for a European hotel chain with multiple brands |
| Utell | Third-party hotel reservations company that needs to update its CRS technology |
| Best Western | Marketing consortium offering a state-of-the-art reservation system to its members |
| TIS | Information-only focused destination management system for the Tyrol region of Austria |
| Gulliver | Comprehensive destination management system that includes multiple routes to the consumer |
| Degriftour | Virtual travel agency that packages and distributes last-minute availability totally electronically |
| TravelWeb | Comprehensive hotel information and reservation Web site leveraging its links with Pegasus's THISCo Electronic Switch to permit direct access to the consumer over the World Wide Web |
| Microsoft Expedia | Comprehensive travel Web site, based on an innovative partnership between Microsoft and Worldspan |
| The Hotel Guide | Hotel list service that is maximizing its investment in data collection by distributing it in print, CD-ROM and Web format |
| Imminus Intranet | Established travel company seeking to create an Extranet for use by UK travel agents for information and reservation purposes |

# Chapter 1

# From Airline Reservations Systems to GDS: the Development of Global Distribution Systems

Once in a great while, a new idea sets off a chain reaction that alters the way people do business. Sometimes, it is a great invention, such as the printing press, the steam engine or the computer. At other times, it appears first as a small convenience. It sneaks up on you while you are asleep, as the Lilliputians did on Gulliver. When you awake, you find your life has changed forever. So it was when the airlines began developing computerized systems to manage their reservations....

Before the development of computerized systems, booking an airline ticket was a complex process. Airlines periodically published their schedules and fares in booklets, which were then distributed to travel agents. If a customer wanted to book a flight from, say, Paris to Berlin, the travel agent had to identify which airlines flew on the required route and examine each of their schedules to see if they had a flight which met the customer's requirements. This process of searching through multiple flight schedules was simplified by the publication of composite directories such as the *Official Airline Guide* (OAG), which consolidated times, dates and prices from multiple airlines into one publication (Bennett, 1996). Once the travel agent had identified a suitable flight, they then had to contact the airline's reservations department to see if seats were available and be quoted a fare. Both the flight details and the fare quoted were then passed on to the customer for approval, after which the travel agent had to contact the reservations department again, reconfirm the details and make the actual booking.

Clearly this traditional three-step process of *searching, calling, booking* was unsatisfactory for all concerned (Emmer *et al.*, 1993). The travel agent had to maintain stocks of airline schedules (which were often out of date as soon as they were published) and also had high telecommunications costs from phoning the airlines to check availability and fares, and again to make bookings. In addition, the amount of time which it took to deal with each customer enquiry, find the relevant information and make the subsequent booking, made day-to-day agency operations very expensive from a labour-cost point of view. Research has shown that travel agents spend up to 80% of their time doing things that prepare them to make a booking, and only about 20% actually making reservations. But, due to the commission system on which the tourism supplier/travel agent relationship is based, it is only this last 20% of time that actually generates any revenue (Heintzeman, 1994). The process was also unsatisfactory from the customer's point of view as it usually involved a considerable delay. The customer also had to trust travel agents to find the cheapest/most convenient flight and fare available, which, given the latter's cost considerations and commission-based method of generating revenue, might not always be the case. Lastly, distribution in this manner was also far from ideal from the viewpoint of the airlines. They had to maintain a large (and therefore expensive) reservation staff to deal with enquiries and to process reservations from travel agents, while at the same time paying commission on each booking. To the airlines, it appeared that they were paying twice for the same work!

## 1.1 The Introduction of Computerized Reservation Systems

The airlines also had a further problem: storing and managing vast amounts of data. Each carrier had to maintain data about flight schedules, fares, seat availability and passenger reservations in order to operate. The sheer volume of data and the rate at which it could change led carriers to turn to computers in the late 1950s. The original reservation programs were developed as internal control systems for the airlines – for use by their own reservation staff to manage seat availability more efficiently (Knowles and Garland, 1994). When dealing with an inquiry from a travel agent, the airline's reservation agent could find information and make bookings quickly and easily using a computer terminal linked to the airline's central database (Archdale, 1993).

Airline managers understood that it would be more effective to allow travel agents to access the central system directly. Therefore, as both computing and communication costs began to tumble in the early 1970s, airlines began to place terminals in their high-volume agencies to allow agents to search for information and make bookings for themselves. Clearly this was far more efficient that the searching, calling, booking process described earlier. Being able to access the reservation database reduced the time necessary for travel agents to both find information for the customer and to make bookings, and also eliminated much of the communication costs associated with the older manual system. It also gave them instant access to real-time availability and pricing information, which helped to greatly increase the quality of their service to the customer. This arrangement was also beneficial from the airline's point of view, as it was less expensive to distribute the equipment facilitating direct access to the system than to hire additional staff to deal with increasing volumes of business. Furthermore, airline managers discovered that travel agents were more likely to book reservations on an airline that supplied them with reservation terminals (Burns, 1995a). This had the effect of increasing market share, aircraft load and attracted incremental passenger revenues, and therefore changed the economies of the initiative from simple cost reduction to one of more strategic importance (Copeland, 1991). Placing terminals in agencies in a way tied agents to a specific airline's flights, thus virtually guaranteeing a future flow of bookings.

## 1.2 Reservations System Operation

As explained above, the primary functions of a computerized airline reservation system are to allow travel agents to find relevant flight information and to make a reservation directly from their terminals without having to telephone the airline reservations office (Klein and Langenohl, 1994). To facilitate this, the major reservation systems provide certain basic functions as part of their system. In addition to displaying the flight details (departure and arrival times, route, classes and fares), and processing the reservation (including seat assignment and the booking of special services such as vegetarian meals or assistance for disabled travellers), most systems provide facilities to handle fare quotations, ticketing and travel agency administration (Schulz, 1996). As fares for flights differ depending on the class, dates of journey, the route, the length of stay and the booking lead time, practically every fare needs to be calculated individually – a time-consuming, complex and error-prone procedure. Automating the process greatly increases efficiency and provides a valuable facility to the travel agent. Additional features which assist in the internal administration of each travel agency (such as, for example, ticket management, invoicing and other accounting functions) have also been added to make the systems more attractive to travel agents (Schulz, 1996).

Owning its own reservation system brought significant benefits to an airline. As we have seen, because of their many operational and cost advantages, CRSs had become almost essential for distribution through travel agencies. Some airlines exploited this to gain a degree of competitive advantage (Knowles and Garland, 1994). A prime example of this was the use of 'display bias' as a marketing strategy. Research has shown that the majority of bookings (75–80%) are made from the first two lines of a list of displayed flights. By listing the flights of their owner airline first, some systems were clearly designed to give preference to the flights of their owner carrier (Bennett, 1996). This was unfair to the smaller airlines who could not afford to develop their own reservation system. Display bias has since been ruled to be anti-competitive and legislation has been introduced to ensure that all flight displays are listed in an unbiased order (Bennett, 1993).

Even without using such tactics, ownership of a reservation system gave other advantages. For example, despite evidence to the contrary, travel agents frequently believed that the flight details, availability and fares of the owner carrier were more complete, accurate and up to date than those of airlines who were merely being hosted on the system. This 'halo effect' meant that travel agents had more confidence in that airline's information and thus were more likely to book their flights (Knowles and Garland, 1994). Owners of airline reservation systems also generated considerable amounts of revenue by charging fees to rival airlines for hosting their flight details on the computer system. This revenue was supplemented by imposing quotas on travel agents to ensure a minimum number of bookings, by charging travel agents a further fixed annual fee for the use of the system and from equipment rental fees (Ernst and Walpuski, 1994). These revenues were so substantial (for example, during the late 1980s, SABRE was showing profits of between 30 and 40% of a total revenue of nearly US$400 million) that Robert Crandall (at the time President of American Airlines) is reported to have said that he would sell the airline before selling the reservation system!

The systems also provide their airline owners with vast amounts of valuable management information, which allows them to track travel patterns, market segment trends and travel agent productivity. This has allowed them to effectively segment the market with complex fare restrictions and to use the principles of yield management to help maximize their profitability (Copeland, 1991). Airlines have also used this data to create innovative marketing programmes, such as, for example, the commission override systems whereby travel agents are paid an incentive to sell a particular airline's seats rather than those of a competitor. These extra commissions are awarded in return for an increase in volume or in market share. For such an incentive programme to be operated successfully, the carriers need a vehicle to monitor and analyse sales patterns, which can only be achieved by using a sophisticated computerized system.

## 1.3 Deregulation of the Airline Sector

In 1978, deregulation of the airline sector in the US gave a tremendous impetus to the growth of CRSs. In essence, deregulation triggered both new airlines and more airlines competing on the same routes. While this ultimately meant cheaper prices for consumers, it also meant more flights, more fares, more limitations and ultimately more confusion. Therefore, the use of a computerized system became essential to try to untangle the complex web of information (Hitchins, 1991). As a result, the first major systems developed in this marketplace. In the US, American Airlines launched SABRE, United Airlines launched Apollo, Transworld Airlines launched PARS, Continental Airlines launched System One, and Delta Airlines launched DATAS II, all in the late 1970s and early 1980s. Growth happened more slowly in Europe, and it was not until the late 1980s, with the threat of replacement by the expansion of the US-based systems and imminent deregulation, that the European airlines began to develop their own systems. In contrast with the US, these were developed and owned by conglomerations of national airlines. Both Galileo (established by British Airways, Swiss Air, KLM and Alitalia and based on Apollo software) and Amadeus (established by Air France, Iberia, Lufthansa and SAS and based on System One software) were conceived in 1987, but did not become operational until 1990 and 1992, respectively. Similar developments occurred in the Asian market, with Quantas and JAL creating Fantasia based on SABRE software, and Singapore Airlines, Thai and Cathay Pacific selecting PARS as the applications software on which to base their Abacus system. (For a comprehensive discussion of the ownership and development of the major global distribution systems (GDS), see Karcher, 1996b, or French, 1998.)

As well as growing in terms of numbers, the airline systems also expanded in terms of functionality. The original systems were airline specific – they only sold flights on their parent carrier. One of the first enhancements was to expand their content to include inventory and fare information from other airlines to facilitate the process of interline ticketing. This was a major change as it greatly expanded the number of destinations to which the system could sell flights. When the systems were airline specific, travel agents could only sell tickets to wherever the owner airline had flights, and had to either change systems or revert to manual methods to process connecting flights. Being able to access a much broader range of flights greatly enhanced the functionality of the systems, changing their orientation from being small and regionally focused to having a more global perspective. The scale of the advantages for all parties was reflected by the speed with which travel agents adopted the systems (Ernst and Walpuski, 1994). They quickly became the dominant instruments for the handling of flight bookings, as can be seen from Fig. 1.1. As a result, the term 'global distribution systems' began to be used to describe these new mega-systems.

However, deregulation also had another effect: the increase in the number of flights led to increased competition, resulting in a reduction in the level of airfares. Travel agents, who receive a fixed commission (usually 10%) on what they sell to the customer, were thus threatened by falling revenues. To counteract this, they began to place increasing emphasis on cross-selling travel products (such as hotel accommodation and car hire) along with airline seats (Knowles and Garland, 1994). Having grown comfortable with the process of booking airline reservations electronically, agents increasingly wanted to be able to source information about and make bookings for other travel products on their computer terminals as well. At the same time, the GDS companies needed to increase their revenue stream. Despite the increase in the number of flights being taken following deregulation, there were simply not enough airline bookings being processed to meet their high operating costs. These two factors prompted them to start using spare capacity to distribute other travel products on their systems (Fig. 1.2; Coyne, 1995). While this was initially limited to car hire, and subsequently hotel accommodation, today's GDS allow agents to find information about and book a tremendous range of products directly from the terminal located on their desk. These include scheduled and charter airline flights, hotel and other forms of accommodation, car rental, package holidays, ferry, railway and bus tickets, cruise packages, yachting, excursions, theatre tickets, and even flowers and champagne. GDS provide the convenience of an electronic 'one-stop-shop' for all travel information and reservation needs, and thus have become an essential channel of distribution for any product sold through travel agencies. Quite simply, if a supplier wants to

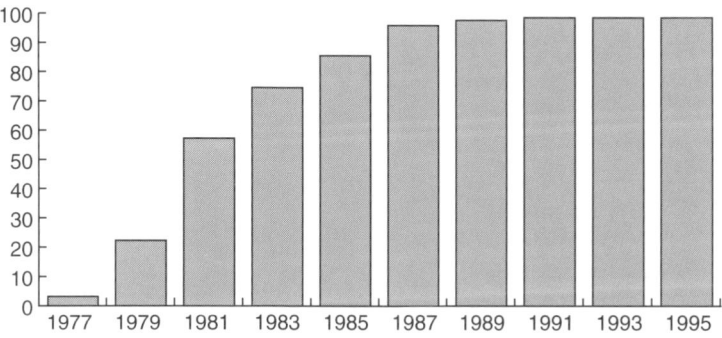

**Fig. 1.1.** Percentage of US travel agents with GDS terminals. Source: World Tourism Organisation

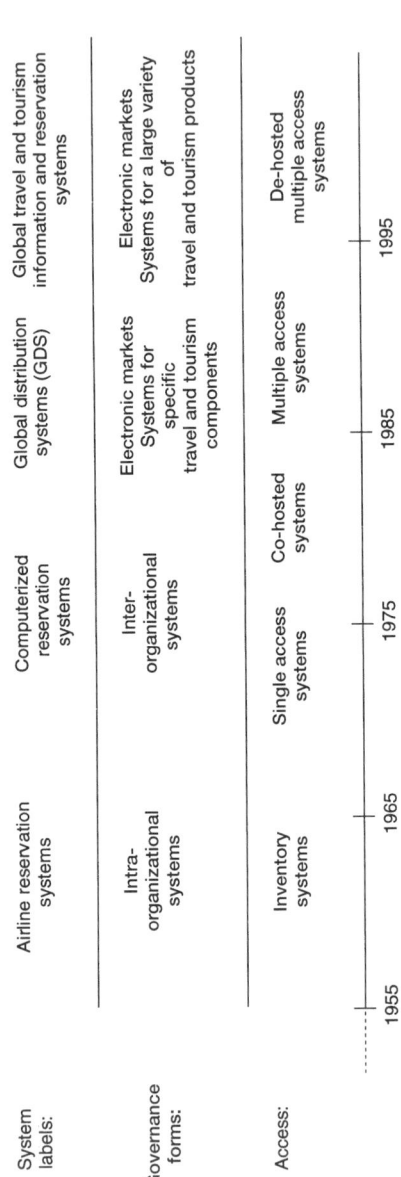

| System labels: | Airline reservation systems | Computerized reservation systems | Global distribution systems (GDS) | Global travel and tourism information and reservation systems |
|---|---|---|---|---|
| Governance forms: | Intra-organizational systems | Inter-organizational systems | Electronic markets Systems for specific travel and tourism components | Electronic markets Systems for a large variety of travel and tourism products |
| Access: | Inventory systems | Single access systems | Co-hosted systems | Multiple access systems | De-hosted multiple access systems |
| | 1955 | 1965 | 1975 | 1985 | 1995 |

**Fig. 1.2.** The chronological development of the GDSs. Source: Karcher (1996a).

be sold by travel agents, they must be listed on a GDS (UFTAA–IHA, 1995).

## 1.4 GDSs Distribute Hotel Accommodation

As was mentioned above, one of the first complementary travel products distributed through GDS was hotel accommodation. Hotels loaded their various room types, descriptions and price categories into spare capacity on the airline reservation system database, and these pieces of information were then available to, and the hotels bookable by, thousands of travel agents worldwide. This was advantageous to each of the participants. Hotels benefited from having their product distributed to a wider audience, travel agents benefited by being able to book a wider range of products through their computer system, and the GDS benefited through increased booking volumes which helped to offset their operating costs.

However, while listing the hotel on a GDS made it available to thousands of travel agents worldwide, it was far from ideal as a sales tool. Problems arose because of the data architecture of the system. As the GDS were originally designed solely to distribute airline seats, their database structure was designed specifically to store information about that product (Emmer *et al.*, 1993). An airline seat is relatively homogeneous – one seat is very much the same as any other on the same route. The hotel product, on the other hand, is very diverse. Even a relatively standardized hotel with a very simple rate structure could have, for example, four room types (suite, double, twin and single) and three rate categories (rack, corporate, leisure), giving a total of 12 combinations (e.g. suite at rack rate, suite at corporate rate, etc.). Of these 12 different rooms/rates combinations, the structure of the GDS database meant that only some of the rates available could be displayed (Wolff, 1996a). This was a major limitation, as the type of rate required is usually the primary decision factor used by travel agents and their clients (Emmer *et al.*, 1993). For example, the client might require a corporate, government or promotional rate, and if one is not listed on the system, the hotel will not be included in the initial search results and thus will be eliminated from further consideration.

The rigid database structure also limited the hotel from a marketing perspective. For example, after the initial search described above, travel agents can 'drill down' to a more detailed description of each hotel that interests them. This second screen is, in effect, like an advertisement (Fig. 1.3), and is particularly important, as this is how a property differentiates itself from its competitors (Emmer and Tauck, 1993). However, the database structure greatly constrained their efforts as it only permitted them to store very limited information about the content of the product itself (Richards, 1995). As a result, the detailed text descriptions necessary to effectively portray a property or to describe a package could not be incorporated into the system (Burns, 1995a). Furthermore, because of the space restrictions, simplified, abbreviated and truncated descriptions often had to be used, frequently to the point where product differentiation and even clarity were sacrificed (Burns, 1995b). For example, room types were described with three-letter codes such as 'A1K'. The 'A' indicated that the room was the best category in the house; the '1' that it had one bed and 'K' that the bed was king size. The best king-sized bed-equipped rooms in every hotel (whether a Ramada Inn or a Ritz–Carlton) were described simply as A1Ks (Schmid, 1994).

Aside from the lack of flexibility, hotels also experienced problems in getting information into the database in the first place. Loading data was relatively technical, as each system used different protocols and syntax and thus each system had to be maintained separately (Knowles and Garland, 1994). In many cases, the data to be loaded already existed in computerized form, but needed to be converted and reformatted to fit the structural requirements of the GDS database. As a result, many hotels used third-party services to handle updates for them, which increased the expense of using a GDS as a distribution channel (Puetz-Willems, 1996). Updating data was also time consuming, resulting in a long lead time between when the hotel wanted to change a piece of data and when it appeared live on the system (Coyne and Burns, 1996). This meant that hotels could not use the GDS as a channel for distributing special packages and promotions unless they were fed into the system several months in advance.

These three problems – the limited number of rates displayed, inadequate descriptions and the lack of special offers – meant that travel agents were not completely confident in the hotel information provided by their systems. In particular, the fact that not all of the rates available in a particular property were displayed led agents to mistrust the computer system, as they were often quoted different availability and prices when they telephoned either the hotel's central reservations office or the hotel directly (McGuffie, 1994). As a

```
DENVER INTL ARPT CO 20FEB-21FEB 1NT 1 ADULT M1
8 HY REGENCY DENVER $6 C 1750 WELTON STREET 22SW L
USD    A1K - 170.00 A2D - 170.00 BUS - 185.00 CLB - 195.00
       COR - 160.00 SEN - 128.00 GOV - 68.87 TVL - 80.00
```

**Fig. 1.3.** A typical hotel listing on a GDS. Source: Emmer *et al.* (1993).

result, travel agents did not use their systems to book hotel rooms to the same extent as with airline seats, and much of the potential of listing hotels on the GDSs was being lost. Although the main GDS subsequently undertook massive renovations of their hotel sales modules to address these problems (see Chapter 5), it was too late. Having struggled for so long to fit multiple rates, varied room types and multiple services into the highly standardized database structure of the GDS, technology planners in both the hotel companies and the GDS agreed that the continued development of the GDS databases to accommodate hotel data would be impractical (Archdale *et al.*, 1992). An alternative strategy was developed. Rather than loading hotel products on to the GDS, separate computerized systems with a database structure more appropriate to the hotel product were developed. These were then linked to the GDS for distribution to travel agents, with a transaction fee being paid to the GDS operator for each booking processed (Schmid, 1994). In this way, the database structure problems discussed above could be overcome while still allowing the hotels to reach the important travel agent market.

## 1.5 Strategies for the Future of GDS

Predicting the future direction of the GDS is a momentous task. In their introductory stages, even the airlines themselves did not foresee how important these systems would become. SABRE was originally envisaged as a seat-inventory system, but at several times during its history has made more profits for its owners than the airline itself. Currently the GDS seem to be concentrating on three main strategies: consolidation, product diversification and market diversification.

Gradually, the major airline-owned GDS have begun to link and merge. This process has largely been triggered by the enormous cost of operating these huge reservations networks (Sheldon, 1995). As with travel agencies, GDS face declining revenues, even though booking volumes are increasing. By merging together and forming alliances (Fig. 1.4), they can create major economies of scale through the creation of centralized databases, which also help to ensure consistency of information. In addition, by having one major global data site, the systems are capable of handling different geographical loading peaks 24 hours a day, and thus using their system to their maximum capacity. New airlines usually choose to rent or buy space on the existing systems, mostly for logistical and financial reasons, but also to reduce the risk of diluting the market by forcing another computerized reservation system (CRS) on travel agents (Vellas, 1997).

Through a series of mergers and take-overs, four major megasystems have emerged; SABRE, Galileo International, Worldspan and

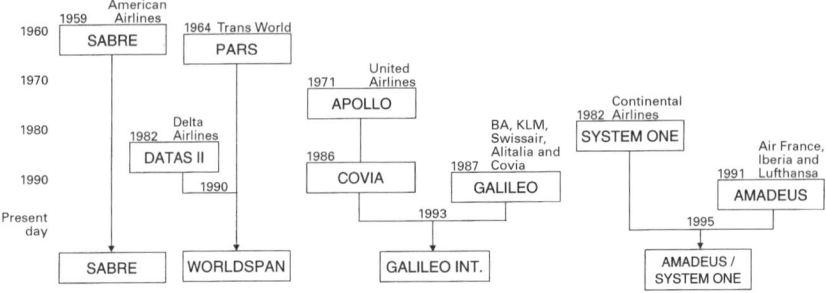

**Fig. 1.4.** The evolution of mega-systems: mergers and acquisitions among the GDSs.

Amadeus/System One. As can be seen from Table 1.1, Amadeus/ System One is the largest system when measured by number of terminals in travel agencies, with 35% of the total number installed worldwide, closely followed by Galileo International with 31% and SABRE with 28% (HEDNA, 1998a). However, big regional differences exist, with SABRE being the dominant system in North America and Amadeus/System One leading in Europe.

Alliances have also been prompted by increased pressure from governments and other regulatory authorities, who seek to separate the systems from their single-airline parentage in order to eliminate the potential for anti-competitive activities. (For example, the European Commission insisted that SABRE establish a European operation trading independently from its American Airlines parent; McGuffie, 1994.) However, divorcing airline and GDS ownership is problematic as many of the economies of scope which accrue from operating both are lost (Knowles and Garland, 1994). A healthier solution may be multi-carrier ownership, as when several carriers operate a GDS (as is the case with the major European systems) they are less likely to behave unethically (Bennett, 1993). Most observers agree that

**Table 1.1.** Regional presence of the four major GDSs, 1997. Source: HEDNA (1998a).

|                | Galileo International | | SABRE | | Amadeus/ System One | | Worldspan | |
|----------------|--------|-----|--------|-----|--------|-----|--------|-----|
| Terminals      | No.    | %   | No.    | %   | No.    | %   | No.    | %   |
| North America  | 15,494 | 30  | 18,783 | 36  | 7,575  | 14  | 9,760  | 19  |
| Europe         | 12,372 | 25  | 5,783  | 11  | 25,777 | 51  | 6,700  | 13  |
| Rest of world  | 8,838  | 32  | 8,887  | 32  | 8,976  | 32  | 955    | 4   |
| Total          | 36,704 | 31  | 33,453 | 28  | 42,328 | 35  | 17,415 | 6   |

the trend towards alliances and mergers is likely to continue, with more and more of the regional systems being incorporated into the mega-systems. Already many regional systems, such as for example Abacus in the Far East, have aligned themselves with one of the mega-systems and are marketed under the larger GDS name. Similarly, SABRE has entered into 'special distribution agreements' with Fantasia in Australia and New Zealand, and with systems controlled by Air India, Indian Airlines, Japan Airlines and China Airlines in Asia, and with Gulf Air and El Al in the Middle East.

Each mega-system's strategy seems to be to dominate the market-place by controlling the highest possible percentage of the world's reservations. Their tactics to achieve this include providing services to as many travel agencies as possible, providing incentives for use of their systems to make reservations, and broadening the range of travel services bookable over their systems. As has been discussed above, GDS now permit access to a broad range of systems administered by, amongst others, car rental companies, sea carriers consortia, bus/rail networks and hotel chains. In addition to distributing travel products, they also provide valuable tourist information (such as destination information and weather reports), support the issue of travellers' cheques, exchange currency, validate credit cards, write insurance cover and automate many of the administratively focused back-office functions of the travel agent (Poon, 1988). In this way, a large bag of services is made available to agencies and – indirectly – to clients, who can secure personal 'turn-key' travel arrangements in a single visit to a travel agency and emerge with all their tickets in their hand. GDSs have also been traditionally focused primarily on business travel and have ignored the potential of the leisure sector. However, they have recognized this imbalance and are working on products which will enhance their leisure booking facilities. This product diversification strategy is particularly important as it makes the systems more attractive to travel agents through giving them the potential to increase their productivity and thus their profitability. The actual systems themselves are becoming more user friendly and more 'regionalized' to help increase sales. For example, displays can now be multilingual, prices can be displayed in local currency and advertising/promotions are targeted to agents in a particular region. Such developments are aimed at making the systems more comfortable for the agent to use, and thus encourage more bookings (Fig. 1.2; UFTAA–IHA, 1995).

The GDS' third strategy is that of market diversification. As we shall see in subsequent chapters, GDS no longer serve solely the travel agent market. Corporate travel departments, meeting planners and wholesalers have joined the more than 350,000 travel agents world-wide who have the capacity to make reservations through a GDS (Gilbert, 1996). In fact, the GDS operators are trying to gain direct access to any business that has enough travel activity to warrant the invasion (Coyne, 1995). Many other forms of electronic distribution are being interfaced with the GDS for information and booking purposes. In addition, the GDS are also actively involved in utilizing new technologies, such as the Internet, to develop distribution channels which will bypass the travel agent and allow consumers themselves to access and make bookings directly from their home or office computer. In short, the GDS are striving to ensure that they continue to play a central role in the distribution of travel products in the future. These efforts, and other developments in the GDS arena, will be returned to in Chapter 5, which examines the future of travel distribution.

# Case Study 1: SABRE

*In a dogsled race, unless you are the lead dog, the view never changes!*

(Bob Crandall, Chairman and President of AMR)

A chance meeting between two Mr Smiths on an American Airlines flight from Los Angeles to New York in 1953 resulted in the development of an innovative computer system that was to change the future of travel distribution. The outcome of the conversation between C.R. Smith, President of American Airlines and R. Blair Smith, a senior sales rep for IBM, was a project called semi-automated business environment research (SABER), which was the first step in the development of today's mighty GDS. Once SABER was operational, the two companies went their separate ways. IBM used their expertise to create PARS, which formed the base technology for the reservations systems of many of American's competitors, while SABER was further developed by American and was re-christened SABRE to distinguish it from the original system.

Prior to the introduction of automation, airline reservations were processed and recorded manually. A system of ticks recorded on coloured index cards was used to control availability on individual flights. These cards were arranged on a 'lazy Susan', and reservation clerks could see the number of seats available on a particular flight by locating its card and counting the ticks. Passenger details were recorded separately as hand-written records, and the entire process was complicated, labour-intensive and unwieldy. For example, a round trip booking from New York City to Buffalo required 12 different people to perform more than a dozen separate steps over a 3 hour period – longer than the flight itself took!

However, the introduction of computerized systems helped to change all of this and greatly improve efficiency and effectiveness. Throughout its history, SABRE went through several separate stages of development.

- SABRE originally took shape in response to American's inability to monitor its inventory of available seats manually and to attach passenger names to booked seats. Thus SABRE began as a relatively simple inventory management tool, although by the standards of the early 1960s, it was an innovative technological achievement. In 1963, the first year it was fully operational, it daily processed data relating to 85,000 phone calls, 40,000 confirmed reservations and 20,000 ticket sales. Over the years, the system's reach and functionality was greatly expanded. Its technology provided the base for generating flight plans for American's aircraft, tracking spare parts and scheduling crews, as it became much more than an inventory control system. But, at the end of the day, this phase of SABRE was still purely internally focused, helping American Airlines to improve the efficiency of its operations.

- The scope of the system changed significantly with the installation of the first SABRE terminal with direct reservations capability in a travel agency in May 1976. Prior to this, American, along with the other major carriers, had been involved in an industry-wide consortium which was trying to develop a shared CRS for use by travel agents. While the proposed system was deemed economically practical, one of American's main competitors, United Airlines, withdrew from the project and announced its intention to place terminals connected to its own reservation system into agencies. Since this would have schedule displays and flight connections biased in favour of United, it represented a competitive threat to the other airlines if it became accepted by the lucrative travel agent sector. As a result, American followed United's example and gave travel agents direct access to their system. Over the decade that followed, SABRE increased the attractiveness of their system for travel agents by adding new services such as hotel, car and rail reservations, incorporating powerful new features to help agents offer better service, and created a comprehensive training and support infrastructure. In terms of airline flights, preference was given to American's services, thus leading to increased booking volumes. SABRE had become a competitive tool, helping to promote American's flights and services over those of its competitors.

- The final stage of development is still in progress today. SABRE has changed from being a single-access system, solely distributing the flights of its parent airline, to being an unbiased multi-access system offering a broad range of travel and travel-related products. American's flights are not treated any differently to those of the other 700 airlines whose schedules and fares are in the system. American Airlines pays SABRE the same booking fees as other airlines, and effectively any benefit which accrues from owning the system has been eliminated. SABRE has become an electronic travel supermarket, acting as a middleman between suppliers of travel services on the one hand and travel retailers, and even the end consumer, on the other. While, traditionally, its strength lay in servicing the business travel market, it has expanded its horizons to the leisure sector in a bid to capture more market share. The company has invested tens of millions of dollars in developing and enhancing its leisure programs, giving users better access to tour operators, cruise lines, ferries, ground transport and railroads, as well as more and more car hire and hotel properties that market primarily to the leisure traveller. Ancillary travel services such as theatre tickets, travel insurance and destination information have also been added, making SABRE more attractive as an all-round tool for travel reservations.

### SABRE Today

Although originally developed by American Airlines, AMR, the parent company of American, separated the SABRE Group from American Airlines, setting it up as a separate subsidiary, on an equal footing with the airline. In 1996, AMR converted SABRE into a public company by offering an IPO (initial public offering) of SABRE Group stock on the New York Stock Exchange. Approximately 18% of the company was sold to public investors. Overall, SABRE is highly profitable, with earnings of $200 million on sales of $1.8 billion in 1997.

SABRE itself is organized into three operating divisions: SABRE Computer Services is the data-processing arm of AMR that developed and now maintains SABRE and its related communications networks; SABRE Development Services is responsible for the development of new products and services to better serve the company's customers; while SABRE Travel Information Network is the marketing arm of the company, which is responsible for selling the system to both travel agents and travel suppliers.

The SABRE core system runs on a very large mainframe located in Tulsa, Oklahoma. This underground facility is designed to withstand virtually anything – earthquakes, storms, floods, even terrorist attack – to ensure that SABRE is kept up and running to provide continuous service to its customers. It processes over 4500 messages and over 65,000 data accesses per second and has data storage capacity in excess of 1800 Gigabytes. It has computer terminals in over 33,000 agencies in 184 countries on six continents, and, in addition to information and reservation services for 750 airlines, it provides services to over 31,000 hotel properties, representing approximately 200 hotel chains, plus rate, booking and availability for over 50 car hire firms. At peak periods, the mainframe system processes approximately 150 million travel requests per day. The group also operates an X.25 network in 76 countries with over 20,000 ports, and this, together with its connections to the numerous travel supplier CRSs, make SABRE the largest private computer system in the world.

SABRE can be accessed in a number of ways by different types of users:

- *Travel agents* are SABRE's core customers and access the system using Professional SABRE. This runs on a wide variety of hardware (from dumb terminals to Windows personal computers (PCs) to mini-computers) and allows agents to check real-time availability and flight information, to reserve travel products and to print tickets. Although most agencies are directly connected to the SABRE system over a computer network, a dial-up version is also available for smaller agencies that cannot justify the cost of a permanent connection.
- *Corporate travel departments* can use Commercial SABRE to access a limited subset of the system's functions. The software is run on a PC and accesses the SABRE core system over CompuServe. Users can check availability and select a seat on a flight that they would like to book. This booking is then routed to their nominated travel agent, who checks the booking, and looks after ticketing and payment issues. In some cases, it is even possible for the ticket to be printed in the corporate customer's own offices using a satellite printed under the control of the travel agency. SABRE also helps companies to better manage their corporate travel budget using its 'Business Travel Solutions' product. This offers reservations capability, as well as expense report processing and post-travel analysis to help a company see, at an individual or consolidated level, just who is travelling, how much is being spent and gauge adherence to corporate travel policies.
- *Consumers* can use services such as EasySABRE on CompuServe or AOL to access the SABRE system. This uses a simple 'fill in the blanks' screen to specify the travel requirements, and the reservation is then transferred to a local travel agency for ticketing and follow-up action. Although EasySABRE's capabilities have now been expanded from solely flights to the full range of travel products available on the full system, its user interface is still quite basic and it has been, to a large extent, replaced by Travelocity (discussed below).

### Innovation at SABRE

From the very beginning, SABRE has been at the forefront of the race to apply technology to travel distribution. As well as being the first computerized airline reservation system, they were among the first to install terminals in travel agencies (experimentally in 1967, fully in 1976) and the first to introduce a frequent flyer programme. Their initial investment in research development and installation of the original SABRE system was almost $40 million (the price of four Boeing 707s at the time) which was considered by industry analysts to be a ridiculous sum to invest in what was, after all, an office automation project.

SABRE has kept this commitment to investing in innovation through technology. For example, it was among the first to provide seamless connectivity to hotel companies, allowing travel agents access to 'up-to-the-minute rate information, room inventory and highly descriptive product information using real time availability directly from the hotel companies own database'. Similarly, it experimented successfully with the use of CD-ROM technology as a sales aid with its SABREVision product (discussed in Chapter 5). According to Robert Teerink, Managing Director, SABRE Europe, the company believes in being proactive, not reactive. He says that SABRE has always tried to be a predictor of trends, and that the key to its success has been its technology leadership. Its uses this leadership as one of its key selling points, and indeed the SABRE system has often been hailed as the supreme example of how excellence in technology use can give a company competitive advantage. This emphasis on innovation continues, with SABRE spending over $90 million on systems development in 1997, with the joint goals of better satisfying its customers and enlarging its market share.

Even with all of this innovation, SABRE is being threatened. Its competitors are forming global alliances, threatening its dominant market position and eating into its competitive advantage. The travel agents sectors in most countries are already well serviced, if not saturated, by the GDS, thus limiting its potential for growth. Non-traditional competitors, such as banks, insurance and technology companies are testing the water in travel distribution and sales, thus further eroding its market share. In order to continue to develop (or perhaps even just to survive), SABRE needs to step boldly into the future – building on the successes of its past, but prepared to change course if the market requires. One advantage that it has over many other companies is its single ownership. This gives it more control over its own destiny and the ability to more easily embark on a chosen course of action than many of its multi-owner competitors.

One of the key strategies chosen by SABRE has been to take advantage of the opportunities presented by the growth in popularity of the Internet. In the spring of 1996, it launched its *Travelocity* service on the World Wide Web, which allows consumers to check availability and reserve travel products directly from their home or office PC, and have their tickets processed and sent to them by mail. This was a good strategic move by SABRE. Although 80% of all airline reservations are currently made through a travel agency, this still leaves a large percentage of travellers who use the telephone to call the airline directly. Giving these customers a method of making their own travel arrangements – in a format that is familiar and easy to use – helps to reduce costs and increase booking volumes. And SABRE does not view it as taking business away from the travel agency, which it sees as its primary customer. Instead it sees it as generating incremental business from a yet-to-be-tapped sector. In 1997, sales from Travelocity and the older EasySABRE service totalled nearly US$100 million, thus indicating the importance of this direct-to-consumer route for the company.

The company has also acted to allay travel agents' fears by helping them to establish their own presence on the World Wide Web. *Web Marketing by SABRE* allows an agency to create its own Web site, with online reservations facilities provided by SABRE. Bookings originating on the Web are passed to the SABRE core system for processing, and then routed back to the agency for ticketing. SABRE has also included a Web browser in its new travel agency platform, Planet SABRE, which allows agencies to tap into the Internet for multimedia information to supplement SABRE. While bookings through the Internet represent less than 1% of overall bookings at the moment, the company recognizes that this will grow substantially as more people come online, and intends to continue to invest heavily in Internet-based technology in the years to come.

# Chapter 2

# Hotel Central Reservation Systems

The growth of travel in the 1960s, which prompted airlines to develop CRSs, put similar pressures on hotels. Individual properties were receiving growing numbers of telephone calls, letters and telexes from potential customers wanting to book accommodation. A clerical squad, often as numerous as that of the front desk, was needed to sort mail, type letters, send telegrams and handle other requests. Bottlenecks were frequent, letter-writing costs skyrocketed and first-class clerk–typists were in short supply (Anon., 1968).

An opportunity for rationalization was recognized by many of the US hotel chains. They noted the inefficiencies of the existing system and determined that the best way to serve the customer, and at the same time provide a valuable service to their member hotels, was to centralize the reservations function into central reservation offices (CROs) (Burns, 1995/96). These functioned in a similar manner to the reservations offices operated by the airlines except, of course, the product being sold was hotel rooms not airline seats. The CRO kept track of the rates, availability, special packages, negotiated rates and descriptions of each property, and allowed customers to book any room in the chain by contacting a single central location. The booking process was further simplified by the introduction of toll-free telephone services in the United States in the mid 1960s, which allowed potential customers to make a single free telephone call to enquire about or book any of the chain's hotels anywhere in the world.

Centralizing the reservation function also brought other advantages. Bottlenecks were reduced while, at the same time, reservations agents were used more intensively than they would be at unit level, as centralization helped to average out the busy and slack periods. A more professional level of customer service was possible through the use of dedicated, well-trained staff, and service quality was also more consistent as centralization made it easier to monitor and control. Overall the lesson was clear: a centralized booking environment was faster, more efficient and, if well designed, far more economical to operate than unit-level reservation offices (Burns, 1996). Only two major costs remained: telecommunications, as the CRO had to pay for the provision of the toll-free service; and the labour cost of the reservations agents needed to answer phones and process other enquiries.

The UK-based budget hotel group Travelodge provides a very good example of how a CRO can operate efficiently. In all its marketing, the group publishes a single toll-free number which connects the customer (be it a travel agent or independent traveller) to a CRO. Individual reservation numbers for each property are not published and individual lodges do not handle advanced reservations, referring all enquiries to the CRO (Schmid, 1994). In this way, reservations staff and operating costs on a group basis are kept to a minimum. This approach has worked very well for the group, with an average of 6500 calls per day for its 120 lodges (HSSS, 1995). Particularly interesting is its philosophy of never being full. Should the particular lodge requested not have rooms available, accommodation is automatically offered at a nearby alternative (Schmid, 1994).

## 2.1 Computerized Reservation Systems

Initially, central reservations agents processed bookings by checking on 'availability blackboards' displayed on the walls of the centre, or in massive books which were updated by hand. However, as booking volumes grew, these manual operating methods were quickly overwhelmed and hotel companies were forced to introduce computers to help manage the increasing workload. The hotel companies were, however, able to benefit from the experience gained in the development of the airline system. Kemmons Wilson and Wallace Johnson, a pair of visionary entrepreneurs, noted American Airlines' success with their computerized system and thought that the concept might work for handling reservations for their young Holiday Inn chain. In 1965, Holiday Inn introduced its Holidex CRS, an innovation often credited with helping to transform what was then a small budget hotel chain into a world leader (Coyne, 1995). Similarly, in the early 1970s, Westin Hotels and Resorts developed a hotel version of United Airlines' Apollo reservation system that it called 'Westron'. This was then licensed to other major hotel chains and became an early industry standard (Schmid, 1994).

The first generation of hotel CRSs suffered from similar problems to those encountered when selling hotel products over GDS. For example, the early systems only held very limited data about each property – basically just the number of rooms available and the rate at which they were to be sold. Updating information was also troublesome and costly, with individual hotels telephoning or telexing the CRO with their inventory status, and the information subsequently being transcribed into the system. While their data were being hosted on the GDS, the needs of the hotel companies had a low priority, as their sales made up such a tiny percentage of transactions (Coyne and Burns, 1996). By developing their own systems, hotel companies gave themselves both the opportunity and the flexibility to make the systems more closely match the requirements of the hotel product (Petitt, 1993). In this way, the new systems could be turned into more suitable sales and marketing tools (Burns, 1995a). The hotel company's initial priority was to eliminate two of the major limitations which had been experienced while hosted on the GDS: the cryptic product descriptions and the limited number of rates which could be displayed by the system.

As was discussed in Chapter 1, GDSs were originally designed solely for processing airline flight reservations. As such, their database structure was limited to storing relatively basic descriptive data, a factor that greatly handicapped their usefulness as a marketing tool for the more heterogeneous hotel product. Similarly, the database structure only permitted a limited number of rates to be displayed, which was a considerable problem given the growing importance of yield management techniques in the hotel industry. In developing their own systems, the hotel companies were able to specifically design the database to overcome these limitations (Burns, 1995b). Free from the constraints of the GDS, the new systems were capable of accommodating extensive product details written in full, abbreviation-free English, along with an unlimited number of rates and room types. These developments made the systems far more effective as both an informative and marketing tool, as it gave the hotelier the opportunity to differentiate based on product quality and features as well as on price (Burns, 1996). Rates that included extra amenities (such as a complementary breakfast), or the constituents of a package deal or other special offer, could now be displayed, as illustrated by Fig. 2.1. This made systems more suitable for addressing the leisure market as they could now cope with describing a more heterogeneous product.

## 2.2 Linking with Global Distribution Systems

Travel agents also benefited from the development of CROs and CRSs. Traditionally, they had used published travel guides such *Fodor's Guides*, the *AAA Tourbook* and the *ABC Guide* to find information

**Table 2.1.** Central reservation systems of major hotel companies. Ranking based on *Hotels*, July 1997, p.48.

| Rank | Hotel chain | Number of hotels 1996 | Number of rooms 1996 | CRS name |
|---|---|---|---|---|
| 1 | Cendant Corp./HFS Inc. | 5300 | 490,000 | (In development) |
| 2 | Holiday Inn Worldwide | 2260 | 386,323 | Holidex |
| 3 | Best Western International | 3654 | 295,305 | Lynx |
| 4 | Groupe Accor | 2465 | 279,145 | ResInter/TARS |
| 5 | Choice Hotels | 3197 | 271,812 | Choice 2001 |
| 6 | Marriott International | 1268 | 251,425 | Marsha |
| 7 | ITT Sheraton Corp. | 413 | 130,528 | Reservatron IV |
| 8 | Promus Hotel Corp. | 809 | 105,930 | HMS II/System 21 |
| 9 | Hilton Hotel Corp. | 245 | 101,000 | Hiltron |
| 10 | Carlson Hospitality | 437 | 91,177 | Pierre |
| 11 | Hyatt Hotels | 176 | 80,598 | Spirit |
| 12 | Inter-Continental Hotels | 193 | 69,632 | Global 2000 |
| 13 | Hilton International | 160 | 51,305 | Hiltron |
| 14 | Grupo Sol Melia | 203 | 47,371 | SolRes |
| 15 | Forte Hotels | 259 | 46,847 | Fortes |

when looking for a hotel to meet a guest's needs and budget (Emmer *et al.*, 1993). While these provide considerable information on facilities, etc., they rarely show room rates, as they are published infrequently and would become outdated too quickly. As a result, travel agents had to contact the hotel directly to determine rates and availability, which usually involved expensive long-distance telephone calls. Thus the advent of the CRO, which provided a toll-free number to find information about and to make bookings in any hotel in a chain, greatly helped to reduce costs and encourage the booking of hotel

```
**HOC INSIDE AVAILABILITY** WELCOME TO HYATT ...COME ON IN
REF USD RATE HY 09962 REGENCY DENVER
1   185.00 RACK/CORPORATE REGENCY CLUB
         DLUX RM W/ KING OR 2 DBL BEDS ON 25TH FLOOR W/
         MOUNTAIN OR CITY VIEWS WORK DESK 25 INCH TV FULL
         BRKFST MON-FRI
2   160.00 RACK/CORPORATE HYATT GUEST ROOM
         SUPERIOR RM W/ KING OR 2 DBL BEDS LOCATED ON
         FLOORS 4-20
3   175.00 RACK/CORPORATE BUSINESS PLAN
         DLUX RM COMP BKFST COFFEE MAKER IN-ROOM FAX
         MACHINE IRON W/BOARD AND BUSINESS CENTRE
```

**Fig. 2.1.** A typical listing on a hotel CRS. Source: Burns (1995b).

rooms by travel agents. However, as travel agents were already familiar with the use of computer systems for information search and booking purposes through their use of airline systems, they increasingly began to demand that hotel rooms be made available in the same way. From the travel agent's perspective, the cost of finding information and processing a booking is much lower when the task is carried out electronically. For example, managers at Thomas Cook estimate that the cost of making a hotel booking over the telephone is approximately £3, as opposed to 76p to reserve the same room electronically. As a result, many agencies are actively discouraging their staff from using manual search and booking methods, and operations not available on their computerized systems will lose out (Welch, 1995). Electronic distribution is also attractive from the hotel company's point of view, as the incremental cost of processing bookings electronically is dramatically less expensive than processing a toll-free call to a CRO (Schmid, 1994). For example, a recent estimate claims that a voice booking, through a CRO, costs hotels between $12 and $15, while the cost of processing it electronically can be as low as $3.50 (HSMAI, 1995).

While many of the processes and data which travel agents needed to be able to book hotels electronically were already present on the reservation systems, it obviously was not feasible to place terminals in each travel agency as had happened with the airlines. The solution lay in developing a link or interface between the new hotel reservation systems and the GDSs. In this way, travel agents could access the hotel products electronically through their existing terminals without encountering the database structure problems discussed earlier, and the hotel chains did not have to make massive investments to develop their own distribution network (Welch, 1995). Several different levels of connectivity are possible. These are differentiated in two ways; by the speed at which they can return a confirmation code to the person making the booking; and by where the data being displayed on the travel agent terminal is actually stored. The lowest level of connectivity is known as 'manual'. In this case, the hotel product descriptions and rates are hosted on the GDS database. Travel agent bookings are handled using a series of manually processed electronic requests and responses commonly known as queues (Emmer *et al.*, 1993). These are basically electronic messages that are sent to a GDS terminal located in the hotel chain's reservations office. The reservation agent examines each booking request, checks availability, makes the booking and returns another electronic message containing a confirmation code back to the travel agent. The speed of response depends, to a large extent, on staff efficiency at the hotel reservations office (Vallauri, 1995). Obviously this is a very basic level of (non-electronic) connectivity which can result in considerable delays for the travel agent, and is also inefficient from the hotel chain's point of view as it involves processing reservations in two places – on the GDS and on their own internal reservations system.

'Type B' connectivity is more advanced in that the process is automated and the travel agent receives a confirmation number directly from the hotel chain's CRS without human intervention. A further enhancement is known as 'type A', where the confirmation is received within 7 seconds. This speedy response means that the travel agent knows that the booking is confirmed while their customer is still present, and thus they are far more likely to book hotels offering this level of connectivity (Welch, 1995). In both of the latter cases, the description data and rates are still stored on the GDS database, with the hotel CRS computer only being contacted to check availability, make the booking and generate the confirmation number. As a result, only the abbreviated descriptions and limited number of rates hosted on the GDS are available to the travel agent.

The highest level of connectivity currently available is known as 'seamless' connectivity. In this mode, the GDS database is no longer used, and all the data displayed on the travel agent terminal has been instantly and automatically extracted from the hotel CRS (Table 2.2). It allows the travel agent to see directly into the hotel chain's CRS – in effect using the GDS as a form of electronic gateway (Burns, 1996). This is a huge step forward as it eliminates the truncated description, limited number of rates and confidence issues discussed earlier. Comprehensive product descriptions can be displayed on the travel agent's terminal, which allows hotels to market themselves based on their product merits, rather than on price alone (Coyne and Burns, 1996). As it draws information from the hotel's CRS, seamless connectivity permits a complete listing of the rates available. This helps to eliminate the mistrust that travel agents have traditionally felt in

**Table 2.2.** A comparison of type A vs. seamless connectivity. Source: Burns (1995/96).

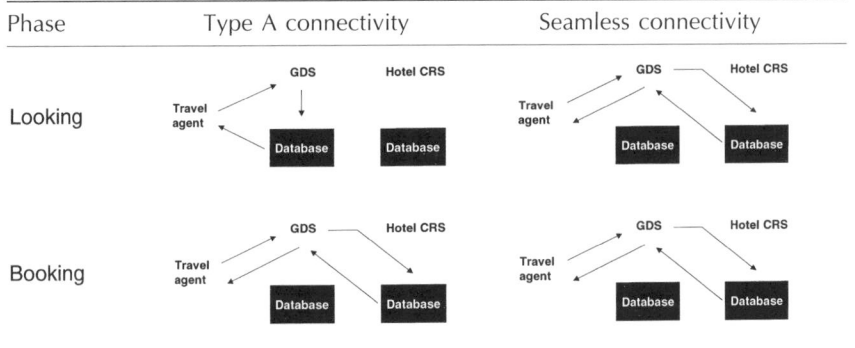

| Phase | Type A connectivity | Seamless connectivity |
|---|---|---|
| Looking | | |
| Booking | | |

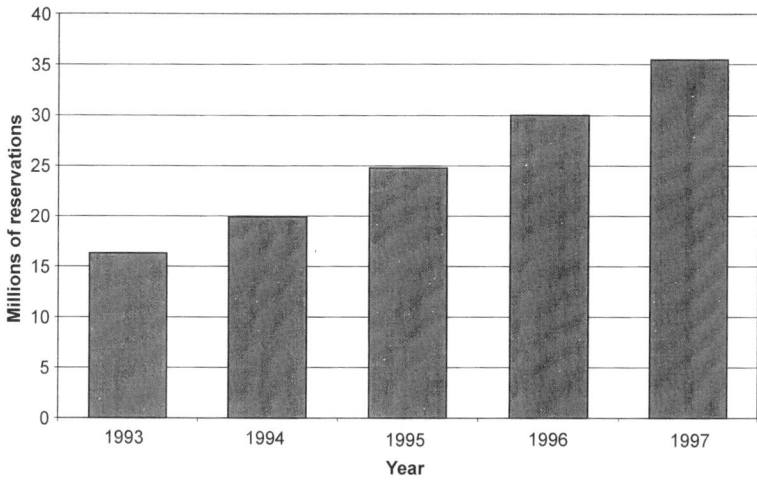

**Fig. 2.2.** Annual net GDS hotel reservations. Source: HEDNA (1998c).

relation to hotel GDS data. Now the availability and rate data shown on their screens are exactly the same as those at the CRO, and thus there is no need to contact the CRO office by telephone in an effort to obtain lower rates (Selwitz, 1993). In addition, seamless connectivity eliminates the problem of updating multiple databases, thus decreasing both costs and the chances of error (Wolff, 1996b). Each of the major GDSs has implemented seamless connectivity on its system. The net result of this and the other enhancements discussed earlier is significant and sustained growth in the number of hotel reservations processed over the GDS (Fig. 2.2).

## 2.3 Switching Companies

As we have seen, connectivity has become a competitive necessity for most hotel chains. Travel agents have rapidly come to expect hotel products to be available on their computerized systems, and are increasingly basing their buying decisions on the detailed information they find there (Burns, 1995b). However, it is both expensive and technical to interface a CRS with the GDS computer systems. Recent estimates put the cost of developing just the software portion of such a link at approximately £175,000 (Ernst and Walpuski, 1994). As was illustrated in Chapter 1, four mega-GDSs have developed, each of which is considerably different in terms of technical requirements and methods of operation. While developing a link with just one of these systems might be operationally and financially feasible for the larger

**(a) Without a switch**  **(b) With a switch**

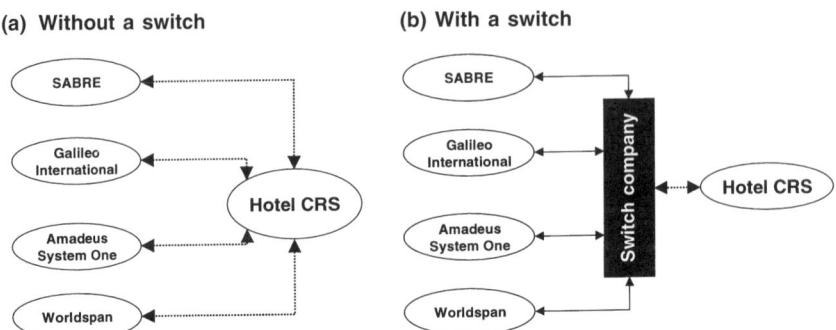

**Fig. 2.3.** The switch company concept. Without a switch company, the hotel CRS has to develop multiple interfaces (shown by the dotted lines) to link with the GDS. Where a switching company is used, only a single interface needs to be developed.

hotel companies, links with each of the big four are needed to ensure maximum exposure in the worldwide marketplace. To achieve this, of course, would be prohibitively expensive as it would entail four times the cost and technical headaches.

A more effective solution has emerged. Two companies; THISCo (The Hotel Industry Switching Company) and WizCom have developed similar concepts of a universal switch (Fig. 2.3). This is not intended to be a CRS in itself, but to act as a bi-directional interface between any major airline GDS and any hotel CRS. Transactions are automatically 'translated' by the switch so that there is compatibility between the systems (WTO, 1995). Therefore, instead of having to build multiple interfaces between the hotel CRS and the airline systems, hotel companies need only develop a single gateway (between their CRS and the universal switch) which allows them to connect to all the major systems. As well as being less technical, such a solution gives access to the vast global marketplace of GDS at a relatively low cost (Archdale, 1993).

## 2.4 Hotel Representative Companies

One of the factors limiting the growth of hotel electronic bookings is that only a particular type of hotel is well represented on the GDS. By and large, all the GDS provide access to the same 30,000 or so hotel properties, which tend to be members of the large international hotel groups (Coyne, 1995). Travel agents, however, need the systems to provide information about all types of hotels – domestic or international, chain or independent, large or small. As Richard

Brooks (senior director of rooms management for Stouffer Hotels) points out:

> Information is the most important commodity a hotel has to give travel agents. By not having an effective state-of-the-art CRS, you severely limit the information you can provide them and consequently their ability to sell your hotel.
>
> (Wagner, 1991)

Thus, there is increasing pressure on small groups and independents to find a way of making themselves available electronically, despite the considerable costs involved.

The dominance of the large groups can, in part, be explained by the prerequisite of having a CRS. HSSS Ltd, a leading firm of UK-based hospitality technology consultants, point out that the start-up cost of even the simplest centralized system is at least £100,000 (HSSS, 1994). Enhancements such as developing interfaces with the GDS increase costs substantially. Even though the benefits of CRS use and accepting electronic bookings are equally as compelling for smaller hotel groups as for the larger ones, such levels of investment are difficult for small hotel groups to justify. The large international chains are able to afford such systems as they have high booking volumes which reduce the per transaction cost, they usually target the business traveller, where high prices mean high margins, and also can spread the cost across the entire chain of properties. Two alternative strategies being used by smaller companies to overcome this problem and gain economies of scale are to band together into a marketing consortium or to outsource their reservations function to a third-party reservations service.

Well-known examples of marketing consortia include SRS Steigenberger, Concorde, Utell, Best Western and Leading Hotels of the World. While most such 'alliances' provide a wide range of services, including advice on marketing and promotion, advertising efforts and sometimes even 24-hour international toll-free central reservation facilities, it is their ability to provide cost-effective access to electronic distribution which is their key selling point (Welch, 1995). Indeed, the benefits of cooperation in this way are so great that it has been cited as one of the principal driving forces behind the growth of global brands (Go and Pine, 1995).

Outsourcing of the central reservations function has become increasingly popular, with, for example, nearly one-fifth of the major international hotel companies outsourcing some aspect of their reservations functions to a third party (HEDNA, 1997). Several different levels of service are possible. The most basic is known as 'generic', where calls to the CRO are answered with a simple 'Hello,

Reservations'. The second option is known as 'private label', and reservations agents respond to calls with the client's name (for example, 'Good morning, ABC Hotels reservations') which helps to retain corporate identity (McGuffie, 1994). In both cases, clients are listed on the CRS, and thus are available to travel agents through the GDS. The client therefore gets the benefits of electronic distribution with a minimum of capital costs. Operational costs are also more predictable as they are generally transaction based. As having access to the latest features is a key selling point when attracting new members, third-party reservation systems also tend to place a lot of emphasis on developing their reservation systems to incorporate the latest technologies. Thus a hotel company can have access to these state-of-the-art facilities at a relatively low cost.

An alternative to using a third-party reservations service is to outsource only the data processing component of the reservation process. In such cases, the hotel operates their own voice reservations centres, but uses computer services owned and operated by an outside company (either a specialist company such as The Alliance or Anasazi Travel Services or another hotel group). The owners of the system generate extra revenue by 'sub-letting' spare capacity on their system, while the renter gets access to electronic distribution facilities without the expense and technicality of purchasing and maintaining a computer system (Anon., 1993). Once again, costs are highly predictable, with expenses based on transaction volumes plus a fixed monthly fee. Limitations associated with using generic display screens and booking functions are balanced by the immediate availability and proven performance of the system, combined with no responsibility for its maintenance and freedom from substantial capital commitment (Burns, 1995a).

## 2.5 The Allocation Issue

A key issue with CRO and CRS operation is where to maintain the room inventory. Most chains have traditionally chosen to let the actual inventory reside at the property level, with an allocation or some sort of free sale status available at the central level that permits bookings to be made. With this system, each hotel makes a certain number of rooms on each date available to the CRO. The central office therefore knows that there are rooms available and does not have to contact the unit to check availability every time there is a booking request (Kasavana and Cahill, 1992). The potential bookings are 'blocked' at the property level and are effectively regarded as already sold.

However, the use of allocations has always been unpopular and problematic. Firstly, hotel general managers have traditionally been reluctant to surrender a portion of their room inventory to the CRO because, at the end of the day, they are ultimately responsible for unit profitability and thus wish to retain control over all aspects of its operation (McGuffie, 1994). Secondly, unless it is very closely monitored, there can be problems with the operation of the allocation system. For example, if a CRO does not manage to fill its allocation, then the possibility exists that rooms can be available while reservations are being denied at the unit level. Similarly, if high occupancies are expected and the unit manager reduces or eliminates the allocation, there is a risk that bookings could be denied at the central level while rooms are still available at the unit level (Troy, 1993). These examples also illustrate the final problem caused by the use of allocations: any blocked rooms are essentially being sold at a predetermined price, regardless of market fluctuations after the allocation was initially made (Castleberry *et al.*, 1998). Data at the central system and the individual property can become out of sync, and customers may find that they can get better rates by phoning the property directly than they can by consulting the reservation system. Therefore the use of allocations does not please anyone. What is needed is a method of ensuring that the availability and rates shown on the system are always the same as those at the unit, thus allowing the central system to sell up to and including the last available room (Knowles and Garland, 1994).

Two different approaches are being investigated as possible solutions to the 'allocation problem'. The first is to develop *bidirectional interfaces* that automate communications between the CRS and the unit level property management system (PMS) to facilitate keeping the two databases in sync (Troy, 1993). When a room night is booked through the CRS, the individual property's database is automatically notified and updated. Likewise, each time a reservation is booked directly at the property, the CRO is updated. As a result, the chances of underselling or overselling a property are significantly reduced. The major limitation with this strategy is that the proliferation of different PMS software used by most hotel groups makes the development of such interfaces impractical. Until each chain chooses and implements a standard PMS configuration in all its units, this arrangement is unlikely to become commonplace.

An alternative, and possibly more efficient, method of achieving the same goal is the use of *single-image inventory* (Burns, 1995b). Instead of having separate reservations databases at the CRO and the unit property level, many CRSs and PMSs are being re-engineered to share the same room inventory database, usually located at the CRO level. All reservations are maintained on the CRS, and arrival details are automatically downloaded to the PMS on a nightly basis. Property-level staff can either access the CRS to process inquiries and take bookings, or else can take advantage of developments in telecommunications technology to transparently re-route the caller to the CRO (Wolff, 1996b). The major advantage of single-image inventory is that since everyone (property-level reservations staff, the CRO and even travel agents through the CRS) is effectively working with the same data, systems can never go out of sync. Thus the last room can be sold equally well at the individual property, at the CRO or even by the travel agents through the GDS. It also has other advantages in that resources are not wasted in maintaining multiple databases. Having to change rates and update descriptions on a variety of different systems is time consuming and, with each additional database, there is increased chance of error (Wolff, 1996b). With single image inventory, information is updated once and available to everyone. The management of reservations at the group level allows some very interesting yield management tactics to be used, particularly where the hotels are located near to one another geographically, and facilitates the collection and maintenance of important management information (HSSS, 1994). A centralized reservations database forms a vast data repository, which offers important opportunities for analysis and reporting. Consolidation of data company-wide allows management to easily track local, regional and global performance, trends and preferences. The latest data mining techniques can be used to compile precise marketing, sales and operational reports, such as, for example, travel agent tracking (by individual hotel, city, region and total corporate), or the warehouse used to support chain-wide guest history/customer loyalty schemes (Coyne, 1995). Not only the upmarket chains are taking advantage of this opportunity: Cendant Corporation, whose brands include Days Inns, Howard Johnson, Knights Inns, Ramada, Super 8 and Travelodge have recently announced details of a $75 million project that will equip each of their properties with a standard PMS connected to a central system with reservations, data warehousing and reporting facilities (Burns, 1998).

## 2.6 Conclusion

Hotel CRSs have developed rapidly from being simple data processing systems into tools essential for marketing and distribution. Today, there is a bewildering array of choices available to the hotelier with regard to electronic distribution, as can be seen from Fig. 2.4 and, as we will see in later chapters, the number of options will increase even further as both intermediaries and suppliers themselves take advantage of the opportunities provided by the Internet.

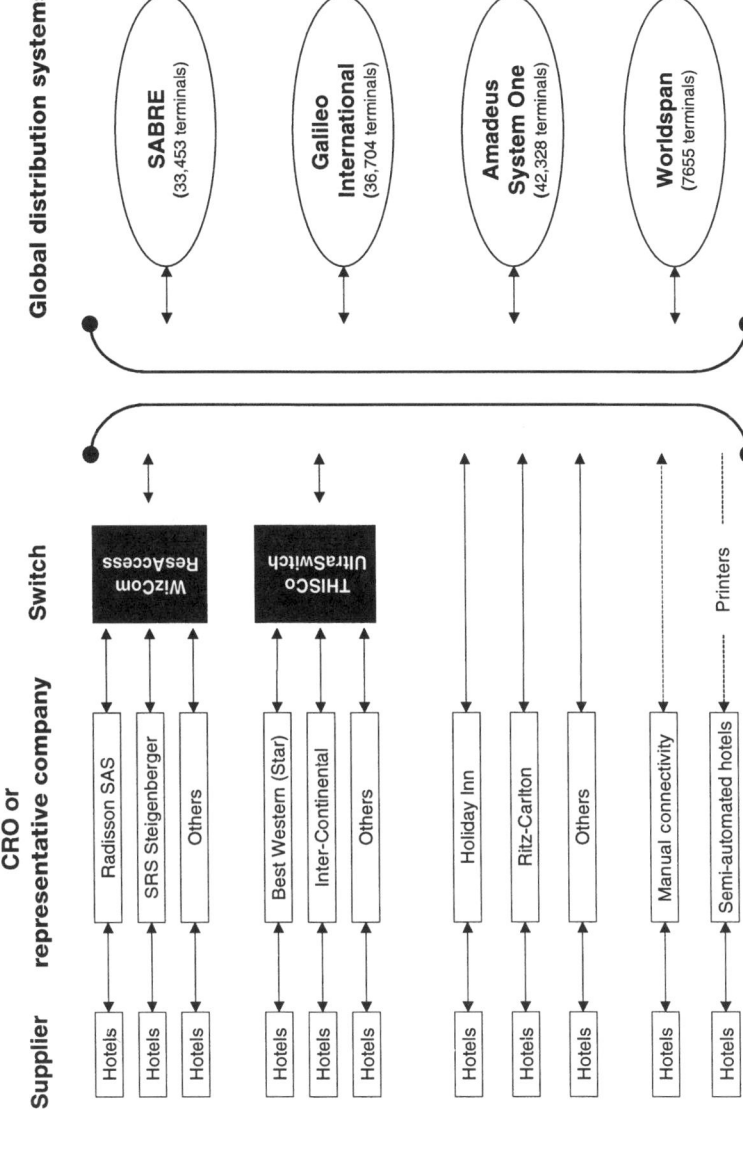

Fig. 2.4. Connecting hotels to the GDS. Source: Emmer *et al.* (1993).

# Case Study 2: Holiday Inn

Holiday Inn is a division of the UK-based Bass Plc and is one of the world's largest single hotel brands. Throughout its history, it has been a leading example of how the use of information technology (IT) can lead to competitive advantage. Key to its strategy is its Holidex CRS, which is widely regarded as the industry's largest and most sophisticated. This system links the 370,000 guest rooms in the more than 2000 properties owned and franchised by Holiday Inn in more than 60 countries with 21 CROs and more than 60 corporate-implant Holidex terminals, as well as with travel agent terminals worldwide through the GDS. More than 70,000 room nights are booked each day through the system – a total of about 25 million a year representing nearly $2.4 billion in revenue for the chain.

Kemmons Wilson developed the idea for Holiday Inn because of what he called 'the most miserable vacation trip of my life'. In the 1950s, roadside lodges in the US were of unpredictable quality and price. Together with his mother, Wilson opened the first Holiday Inn, near Memphis, Tennessee, featuring large rooms with two double beds, a restaurant and a swimming pool. From the start, Holiday Inns were designed to appeal to families travelling by car. They offered larger rooms than competitors and free television, free ice and a telephone in every room. The chain expanded rapidly, outstripping Wilson's ability to raise capital. Consequently, to keep up with demand, Holiday Inn began selling franchises in 1955.

In operating franchises, Holiday Inn ensured that they applied strict operating standards and supplied franchisees with almost everything, apart from the land upon which the hotel would be built, in order to ensure that there were 'no surprises'. This was the beginning of a chain that was to make its reputation on universality, quality and consistency and, as Teare (1993) notes, 'the original Holiday Inn concept or 'core brand' gained international recognition for setting and achieving consistent high standards in product design and service'.

In the hotel franchising business, the development of the franchise network is the critical factor. Since each additional property in the hotel chain is financed by the franchisee, who also pays both a franchise fee and royalties, the parent company or franchiser is able to spread fixed costs over a larger number of franchisees. A critical mass

This case study was prepared by Peter O'Connor, Assistant Professor, Institut de Management Hôtelier International (IMHI), as a basis for discussion rather than to illustrate either effective or ineffective handling of an administrative problem.

of franchisees allows the franchiser to maintain training and advertising departments, functions in which independent hoteliers seldom excel. Last, but not least, each additional franchised hotel exposes the franchiser's brand name in a new geographical market, creating the potential to build referral business for other hotels in the system. However, the sector is very competitive, with many choices for the potential owner or franchisee. With each franchiser offering enticing deals, its no wonder that there were close to 2200 flag changes in the US in 1996 alone. To be successful, franchisers must offer added value to their prospective clients – something a little more than their competitors. In Holiday Inn's case, one of the key components of its benefits package is its sophisticated use of technology to aid in marketing and distribution. Advertisements for Holiday Inn franchises specifically focus on the strengths of the Holidex reservations system, and point out that if hotels want to benefit from them, 'it's time to talk franchising'.

## The Holidex System

Holiday Inn has traditionally been at the forefront of the application of technology to the hospitality industry. The original Holidex system was developed in the mid-1960s, and was based on dumb terminals. The system has obviously been considerably enhanced and developed over the last three decades, until today where it is based on modern client-server technology. Holiday Inn has controlled every aspect of the system, building it specifically to meet the needs of the company. While this has resulted in the system being very expensive, both to build and to operate, it has also made it highly successful, delivering nearly one-third of Holiday Inn's company-wide reservations. The system is also claimed to increase occupancy – giving Holiday Inn properties occupancy rates up to 10% higher than competitors in comparable locations.

The Holidex system itself runs on a mainframe based in Atlanta, Georgia. A mainframe approach is necessary at the central level because of the sheer scope of the system (on average, Holidex processes 350,000 transactions – representing 8000 bookings and $1.3 million in revenue – every hour). The central system is connected by a satellite-based communications system to PC-based clients in Holiday Inn properties worldwide. This network permits a two-way interface between the individual properties and the Holidex system. Where properties have a compatible PMS, information and reservations can be uploaded to the central system, and reservations downloaded in the opposite direction, thus ensuring that the two reservation databases are always in sync. According to Rodney Duckett, manager of Holiday Inn's franchisee-service delivery organization, this allows tighter control over inventory. When a room night is booked through the CRO, each hotel in the system is notified of it. Likewise, each time a room night is booked directly at a property, the CRO gets that information and distributes it systemwide. 'In either scenario, the chances of underselling or overselling a property are greatly reduced'.

Holidex is unusual in that it features a direct connection to many of the major GDSs. Although involved in the initial development of THISCo, Holiday Inn withdrew from the consortium in December 1992. The company felt that it has sufficient technological expertise and business volume to link to the GDSs themselves in a more efficient and cost-effective manner than was possible through THISCo. It also felt that it gained little competitive advantage from using THISCo services because everyone was effectively the same. It thus developed its own links to the SABRE, Apollo, DATAS II and PARS systems, and, according to the company, sells more rooms via GDS than any other hotel company. 'We are the world's largest hotel company', claims Simon Todd, Vice President of Worldwide Sales, 'and we want to be in a position where we are market leaders. The only way we can do that is by being on our own, not developing everything at the same pace as every other hotel company in the system'.

According to Bryan Langton, Chairman and CEO of Holiday Inn Worldwide, 'Our strategy is to focus our resources on systems that will increase the gap between Holiday Inn and our competitors'. With this objective in mind, Holiday Inn is introducing new technology at a cost of $81 m over 6 years that will give further benefits to company properties. The new system, known as the 'Worldwide Hotel System'

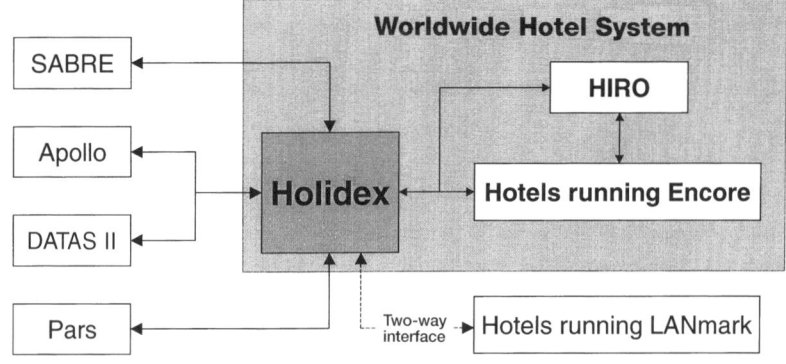

**Fig. 2.A.** Holiday Inn's Worldwide Hotel System (WWHS).

(WWHS; Fig. 2.A) is made up of three components: (i) Holidex; (ii) property management equipment provided by Atlanta-based Encore Systems Inc.; and (iii) HIRO, which stands for 'Holiday Inn Revenue Optimizer'. The Encore software interfaces directly with Holidex, providing real-time communications between each property and the central system, thus permitting sales down to the last available room. Such integration is necessary for the efficient operation of HIRO, which is designed to help maximize revenue at the property level.

HIRO is a very sophisticated retail-pricing model, which calculates optimum room rates for any individual property. It uses the principle of continuously recalculating 'hurdle prices' to arrive at a minimum acceptable rate for each guest stay, taking into account factors such as type and distance away of its competition, the property's own location, the price sensitivity of its guests, booking lead times and levels of occupancy. By continually analysing data fed into it from Holidex, HIRO can closely predict the occupancy of a particular hotel on a given day and the relative daily worth of each room. Thus, in order to operate, it needs an accurate, up-to-date picture of the reservations situation in each unit, hence the need for the integration between Holidex and the systems operating at the property level.

HIRO is unlike other yield management systems in that it is the first to offer an integrate automated length-of-stay optimization. 'Most systems accept reservations based on rate or room availability. The HIRO software allows the hotel to examine these options and adds length of stay as a third consideration' says Trevor Jones, Senior Vice President of Corporate Development. 'In the past, a caller who wanted to stay 3 nights at a certain rate might be closed out if the system showed no rooms available at that rate for one of the nights. That translated into lost business.' (For example, in August 1991, 81% of multiple-night requests to Holidex were turned down because of no availability on one of the nights.) 'With HIRO, the reservation clerk has access to all rooms, at all price points, to give guests the room nights they need. As a result, a hotel might end up with a guest – and revenues – for three nights instead of none.' Initially only applied to centrally made bookings, a property-based version of HIRO has now been rolled out to US properties, where it is reported to be delivering a 3–3.5% increase in revenue. Integration of the system with LANmark (their European-standard PMS from Sulcus) is due for beta test in Europe by the end of the year.

One of the key benefits for the Holiday Inn Corporation is that WWHS allows them to maintain much tighter control over their business. Every reservation that is taken by the hotels within the group flows through the central Holidex system, thus allowing corporate management to have a total picture of what is happening worldwide. And, since the franchiser's revenue depends on the performance of each of the properties, the use of a centralized computerized system allows them to monitor more accurately the true state of operations in each of the properties. The integrated system also allows Holiday Inn to more effectively manage its various marketing programmes.

> By asking our customers a few simple questions when they check-in, and compiling that information through our hotel management system, we can see which marketing programmes are working and which aren't. Through our Priority Club programme, we already know quite a bit about our frequent guests; with this system, we're learning the demographics of our infrequent guests as well. We feel so confident that this system will provide tremendous benefit to Holiday Inn as a company that our MIS organisation is providing each hotel with a front desk platform – including hardware, software and training – at no cost to the property.

> (Richard Smith, Senior Vice President of IT
> for Holiday Inn Worldwide)

# Case Study 3: Groupe Accor

Beginning in 1967 with just a single hotel in northern France, Groupe Accor has grown to become one of the largest lodging, restaurant and travel companies in the world. As of January 1996, Accor operated over 2400 hotels with over 270,000 rooms. Accor employs over 120,000 people in 126 counties around the globe, and is also involved in restaurants, contract catering and, through partnerships, in car rental agencies and travel agencies. The group's total sales volume in 1995 was approximately 31 billion francs (roughly \$15 billion), yielding a EBIT (earnings before interest and tax) of 2.9 billion francs. Approximately two-thirds of this profit was generated by the group's hotel activities.

## Accor Hotels

The hotel industry is not a single market, but is composed of distinct segments, ranging from upscale, luxury hotels down to budget operations. Accor is relatively unique in that it operates across the entire spectrum of the industry in practically every segment (Box 2.A). Its 'Sofitel' brand services the more upmarket customer, 'Novotel', 'Mercure' and 'Ibis' brands are aimed at the mid-price market while 'Etap Hotel', 'Formule 1' and 'Motel 6' target the economy customer. The major characteristics of each of Accor's major brands are shown in Table 2.A.

### *Electronic Distribution of Accor Hotels*

Given its importance as one of the world's largest hotel companies, Accor has a comprehensive central reservations department, encompassing both a worldwide network of telesales centres (with offices in Amsterdam, Evry, Frankfurt, London, Madrid, Milan, New York and Perth) and a computerized reservation system known as 'ResInter' (Fig. 2.B).

As can be seen from Fig. 2.B, this is connected to all of the major GDS via the WizCom switch, services the information and booking requirements of the telesales centres, and is accessible directly to the

**Box 2.A.** Brand characteristics of Groupe Accor hotels.

*Sofitel* is Groupe Accor's upscale product, with 100 hotels in prime locations in leading business and leisure destinations in over 40 countries. It targets an international business and leisure clientele that is looking for a pleasant environment, high-quality facilities and personalized service.

*Novotel* encompasses 305 properties in 50 countries and is positioned at the upper end of the mid-priced category. It targets business clients during the week and the leisure market during weekends and holidays.

*Mercure* again focuses on the mid-price traveller in both business and leisure markets, but offers a more limited service than its Novotel cousin. The brand has 320 hotels in 30 countries, but is mainly focused in and around Europe, and encompasses three different categories (Grand Hotel Mercure, Hotel Mercure and Relais Mercure) depending on comfort level, price and location.

*Ibis* is the largest European hotel chain, with 404 properties including 293 in France, 46 in Germany, ten in Portugal, eight in the UK and a growing presence in the rest of the world. Usually located in city centres, along major roads and near airports, the brand is focused on the mid-priced market, offering travellers quality service at attractive prices.

*Etap Hotel* is positioned at the top of the economy sector, with basic, functional and clean lodgings at very low prices. Each room has an en-suite shower and toilet, can sleep up to three people and has a television. No restaurant facilities are provided, and units are usually located on major roads or at major intersections.

*Formule 1's* concept is practically identical to that of Etap Hotel (basic accommodation at very low prices). However, rooms do not have en-suite facilities, and only have one bathroom for every four rooms. Again there are no restaurant facilities, and properties are located along major roads.

*Motel 6* is once again a budget concept, offering cheap, no-frills accommodation along major roads in the US market.

public over both the Minitel Videotext system and the Internet. However, in the latter case no rates are displayed on the system and the customer can only make a 'reservation request' which must then be processed manually at the CRO and a response sent by Email. ResInter can process reservations for up to 405 days in advance, and handles 19 different room types and 62 different pricing levels for the

**Table 2.A.** Groupe Accor hotels. Source: Accor Annual Report (1995).

| Brand | Hotels | Bedrooms | Grade |
|---|---|---|---|
| Sofitel | 100 | 18,472 | 4 star |
| Novotel | 305 | 47,126 | 3 star |
| Mercure | 299 | 35,279 | 2, 3 and 4 star |
| Ibis | 404 | 41,777 | 2 star |
| Etap Hotel | 87 | 6,016 | Economy |
| Formule 1 | 310 | 22,231 | Economy |
| Motel 6 | 759 | 85,793 | Economy |
| Other brands | 114 | 11,562 | Various |

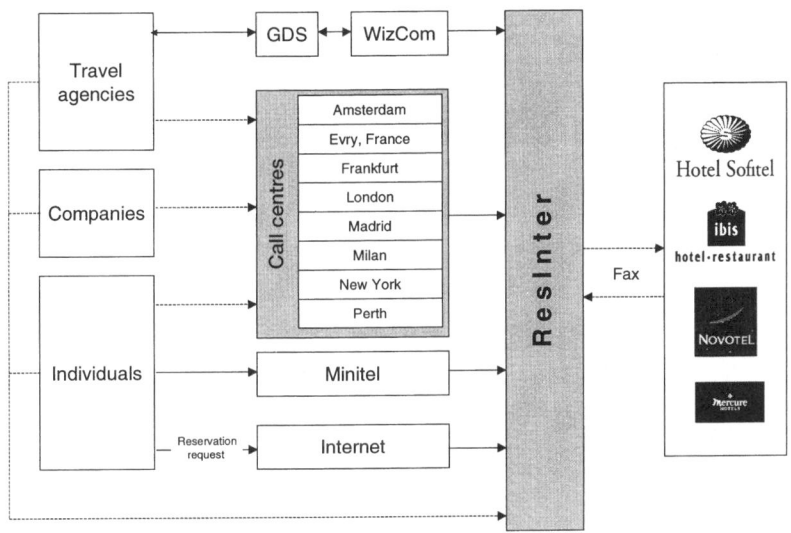

**Fig. 2.B.** ResInter, Accor's central reservation system.

1235 hotels available on the system. During 1996, it processed bookings for nearly 2.5 million room nights, of which 1.3 million originated over the GDS and the remainder through its other channels (Table 2.B).

Despite the comprehensiveness of the system, it is only responsible for processing a small percentage of the group's reservations. As can be seen from Table 2.C, the vast majority of Accor customers still book directly with the hotel. As a result, there is great potential for cost savings by encouraging more use of centralized and electronic routes.

**Table 2.B.** Source of reservations for ResInter.

| Route | Percentage |
| --- | --- |
| Travel agents | 71 |
| Tour operators | 8 |
| Companies | 9 |
| Individuals | 12 |

**Table 2.C.** Source of reservations for Groupe Accor.

| Route | Percentage |
| --- | --- |
| Electronic routes (GDS, Minitel) | 3 |
| Telesales | 2 |
| Direct to hotel | 95 |

### Challenges for ResInter

Accor has traditionally had a philosophy of decentralization. In the view of the founders, the role of top management is to liberate their employees so that they can do their jobs, rather than constrain them with tight management control. Such an approach is in contrast to the emphasis on centralization and reliance on hierarchy that typifies the US hotel industry. Nowhere was this more noticeable than in the operation of their reservation system.

ResInter sells its hotels based on the 'allocation' method. Hotels inform their nearest central sales office of the number of rooms that they have available for sale by ResInter on each date in the future, along with the rate at which they are to be offered. These rooms are effectively regarded as sold at the individual property level, although they can be taken back and the date 'closed out' nearer to their consumption date. Problems arise because availability, rates and reservations are being managed at two separate, remote locations. With an effective communications system, these two inventories can be synchronised. However, with the ResInter system, all communication between the central system and the individual properties (and vice versa) is carried out by fax. Hotels must fax the sales office to modify allocations or rates, and reservations are also sent to the properties by fax. As a result, there is much duplication of effort, particularly in manually updating the computer systems at either end, and errors often occur, resulting in the systems becoming out of sync.

A more appropriate solution would be to have an interface between ResInter and the PMS at each property. However, in Accor's case, creating such a link would be difficult because of the diversity within the chain. A wide variety of different hardware platforms, operating systems and PMSs are being used throughout the group, depending on the size of the property, its brand, its location and even on the preference of the general manager. In addition, many of the smaller properties are not automated at all and thus would still need to use the fax-based system.

Another key issue is how to distribute the budget brands. Despite their image, the budget sector is especially important for Accor, contributing 1035 million francs to EBIT, compared with only 882 million for upscale hotels. However, the three budget brands – Etap Hotel, Formule 1 and Motel 6 – are not distributed electronically (apart from over a dedicated system on the Minitel in France). The justification for this is that their markets are mainly domestic (which are not well serviced by the GDS) and, in any case, their profit margins are too low to support the commissions and fees associated with electronic distribution. However, given the growing competition in this sector, and the importance of the budget market for the profitability of the group as a whole, there is a desire to make these properties as accessible to the marketplace as possible.

Accor has realized the growing importance of electronic distribution for all of its hotels. Philippe Brizon, Chairman of Novotel, has been quoted as saying that 'the hospitality industry is experiencing a real revolution in terms of channels of distribution, and strategically it is about time for us to get equipped'. To that end, Jean-Marc Espalioux, Accor's new CEO, has made technology one of his top priorities and allocated a 500 million franc budget over 3 years to an investment programme with the aims of improving service, increasing efficiency and controlling costs by upgrading and refining Accor's management and reservation tools.

# Case Study 4: Utell International

Utell International is the largest hotel representation company in the world, handling more than 3.5 million hotel reservations and generating US$1.4 billion in reservation revenue annually. It is owned by the Reed Travel Group (part of Reed Elsevier, the UK's largest publishing and information company), which is involved in a wide variety of travel/tourism-related activities, including the publication of the *Official Airline Guides* (OAG), the *ABC Hotel Guide* and the *Hotel and Travel Index*.

Although perceived by many to be a hotel chain, Utell does not have franchise agreements or management contracts with any of its members, neither does it attempt to brand them. Instead it acts solely as a third-party reservations and marketing consultant. It represents approximately 6500 very diverse hotel properties in more than 180 countries. These range from budget to de luxe, city centre to resort, individual independent hotels to hotel chains, including major international brands. Utell proudly boast that 'there is hardly a city centre anywhere in the world where we cannot offer a choice to the customer'.

Utell's prime function is to undertake marketing activities for its member hotels worldwide. As Mike Hope, President of Utell International, explains:

> A lot of our members are independent hotels, who don't have the resources, either of capital or of technological expertise, to help them realise the opportunity of electronic distribution. Utell helps these hotels be at the forefront of marketing exposure and reservations distribution by providing electronic links between its hotels and the world's travel agents.

The company is very successful at what it does. It has doubled its reservations over the past 4 years while its portfolio of members has remained relatively static, thus in effect substantially increasing the number of reservations processed for each property. It attributes this success to its ability to maintain a comprehensive database with up-to-date information on the properties it represents, their prices, location, facilities and availability, and to effectively distribute this information to the travel agent.

This case study was prepared by Peter O'Connor, Assistant Professor, Institut de Management Hôtelier International (IMHI), as a basis for discussion rather than to illustrate either effective or ineffective handling of an administrative problem. All rights reserved.

## Background

Hank Utell, who worked as a journalist in the US during the 1920s, founded Utell. As a result of his chosen profession, he travelled extensively throughout the USA, and thus became familiar with different hotels in each location. Friends and colleagues often asked him 'If I'm going to city X, where should I stay?' Being a true entrepreneur, he saw an opportunity and realised that providing such information could be commercially viable.

At the beginning of the 1930s, Hank approached hotels and struck a deal whereby he would recommend the hotel, in return for which they would pay him a commission. From this informal beginning, Utell developed into a company that provided information to travellers, initially by letter and then, as technology developed, by telegraph and eventually by telephone. As the company grew, it began storing the ever-increasing volume of information about each hotel on microfiche, but these quickly went out of date, as rate and availability information changed frequently. As a result, Utell began to take advantage of development in CRS technology, and developed their own computerized system (known as HANK – *Hotels Automated Network Knowhow*) and interfaced it with the major GDSs. Thus by joining Utell, a hotel could gain both a central reservation centre and make itself available electronically to travel agents around the world in a single step.

## System Operation

Utell operates its reservation service on what is known as a 'freesale' basis. This means that Utell can sell rooms for any date unless the hotel has specifically told them otherwise (known as 'closing out' the date). It is a fundamental principle of the hotel's contract with Utell that reservations made in accordance with the information supplied by the hotel must be honoured.

All information relating to a hotel (where it is located, how many rooms it has, what landmarks are nearby, as well as its rates and availability) are stored in a computer system, known as Unison, for distribution to the marketplace. Hotels can receive reservations and update their data in one of three ways: via telex/fax, via the UtellLink System or via their own CRS system through THISCo's 'UltraSwitch'. Using telex/fax is quite laborious, as the hotel cannot see its current status on each date and thus has to maintain a separate manual system to track which days/room types are open or closed. With the UtellLink, however, the hotel can dial into the system using a modem to see their status and rates for each date. They can perform updates by sending an electronic message to Utell, who will process it and make the appropriate changes on the database. Plans are in progress to develop interfacing with the major PMS, to allow such updates to be performed automatically, but this facility is not available on the current system. As a result, hotels have to monitor reservations data in two places; on their own PMS and on the Utell system.

Utell charges hotels £300 per month for full membership, which gives a hotel full participation in all of Utell's systems and promotions. Utell are also charged $3 per transaction by the GDS, which is passed on to the hotel along with its own 7% commission on each booking. Where a travel agent is involved, another 8–10% (depending on the particular hotel's policy) needs to be paid, thus making the cost of distributing over the Utell system potentially very high. However, the advantages are great, particularly for the small or independent hotel. All Utell screen displays are neutral and unbiased, and therefore such hotels are able to compete on a level playing field with the giants of the industry.

Utell's main route to the marketplace is through travel agents, which account for 95% of all bookings made. (The remainder comes directly from customers, although Utell does not actively promote this route.) As a result, it is important that Utell provides appropriate facilities to allow agents to make reservations by whichever means they prefer. It primarily focuses on the business market, with approximately 90% of its reservations being business-travel related. It also mainly deals with international bookings. As Mike Hope explains:

> If a traveller want to go to a city in their home country, they can book their own hotel, because they usually recognise the hotel name, or at least the name of the group. However, when travelling abroad, booking a hotel becomes less easy. A travel agent can book the flight, but the chances are they won't be able to recommend a hotel. When the agent contacts Utell, that problem is solved. We ask the travel agent some questions: 'Which city do you want', 'What part of the city', 'How much does the client want to pay'. We then take our 6500 hotels and narrow them down to three or four. These can then be described in greater detail until a suitable one for the customer is found. The booking can then be made and a confirmation number given immediately.

Thus Utell forms an interface between the travel agent and the hotel market – 'a sort of travel agent for the travel agent'.

Although Utell maintains a network of 48 international sales and reservations offices to deal with telephone sales, travel agents can also access the service through their GDS terminals to search for suitable hotels, check availability and rates, and make bookings. Unison offers 'Type A' connectivity, which means that an agent making a booking anywhere in the world receives confirmation within 7 seconds. Utell promotes hotels to the travel trade by stressing the UI (Utell International) code. Searching for a hotel in a particular location, the agent simply adds the suffix 'UI' for a list of all hotels represented by Utell in that area. Booking a Utell hotel means that the agent is sure to receive their commission payment. This is facilitated by Utell's *Paycom* and *Paytell* programmes, which allows agents to deduct their commission at the time of booking or, if the clients prefer to settle their own account upon arrival at the hotel, to receive payment through their nearest Utell office. In either case, payment is both guaranteed and timely. By providing facilities like these, Utell is trying to consolidate its position as an intermediary, by providing benefits to both the hotelier and the travel agent.

Although this service is available through all the major GDS, the actual volume of bookings made in this way has remained relatively small. Reasons for this include the limited number of rates offered over the system, as well as training difficulties. To effectively use the system, travel agents must be both trained in and familiar with the hotel reservation system codes and interface. Research has shown that many travel agents cannot even use the normal airline interface of their terminal effectively, and thus often do not know how to access, find and book hotel products over their GDS terminals. An alternative distribution channel also used by travel agents is Videotext systems, such as Hotelspace in the UK or Esterel in France. Although basic by today's standards, these systems have the advantage of being far more user-friendly than the GDS, and thus more likely to be used effectively by travel agents. However, even including those which flow through the Videotext channel, at most 30% of Utell's booking volume comes through electronic routes, and therefore its telesales centres are essential, despite the substantially higher costs involved in processing transactions (Fig. 2.C).

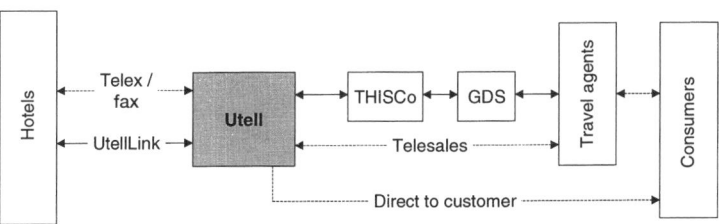

**Fig. 2.C.** Utell International.

Irrespective of the actual distribution channel used (telesales, GDS or Videotext), all transactions feed back into Unison to find information and make bookings. Therefore this reservation system is crucial to the operation of the entire company, and its efficiency affects the ability of Utell to service its customers' needs.

### The Challenge for Utell

Utell was one of the first hotel representative companies and is now the world's largest. Since its creation, Utell has consistently been at the forefront of technology and related commercial developments in the business of making hotel reservations. As has been discussed above, its Unison reservation system is at the core of its business. According to Sally Hurst, Director of Sales and Marketing for Utell, it allows the company to provide quality service, reliable information and secure delivery of bookings and thus its development and management are fundamental to the company's success as a reservations provider.

However, by early 1995 Utell's existing system was increasingly seen as outmoded. It could only store a limited number of rates for each property, could not provide facilities such as seamless integration or interfaces with hotel PMSs and was not capable of permitting bookings over the developing World Wide Web without substantial redesign. As a result, Utell was in danger of losing its competitive advantage in the field of hotel distribution. To overcome this, it began working closely with IBM's Worldwide Travel Business Unit in March 1995 on a major project to develop a new central reservation system, with a budget of approximately US$22 million. The proposed system would take advantage of the latest developments in CRS technology and would feature an unlimited number of room rates, offer last room availability, enhance the commission payment system and provide hotels with better quality sales and marketing data. Furthermore, the system would be designed to use a non-proprietary, open system architecture, and the software was to be developed using a combination of 4GL and CASE tools, which would permit both rapid development and flexible extensions to the core project without affecting the base infrastructure. This would allow Utell to take advantage of any new distribution channels that became available without having to redesign their entire system. Utell even claimed that its delay in developing a new system would be advantageous as it meant that they could learn from everyone else's mistakes and shortcomings, and thus create the perfect system based on everyone's 'wish list'.

Unfortunately, after 18 months of trying, the attempt to develop the system with IBM was abandoned. This represented a major set-back to Utell, whose existing CRS had already been outdated at the beginning of the project. After such an additional period of time, particularly one in which the pace of technological change has increased greatly in the hospitality sector, the lack of a state-of-the-art computerized system represented a serious strategic disadvantage for the company.

In an attempt to limit the damage, Utell made all its 6500 properties available on the World Wide Web on Pegasus's TravelWeb site. This represented a major change of direction, as they originally intended to develop their own Web site (to be known as HotelBook (www.hotelbook.com), which would have booking capability as soon as the new reservation system came online. However, the lack of a modern CRS once again limited Utell's effectiveness, as it could not take advantage of TravelWeb's main selling feature – online booking – until it upgraded its reservation system.

# Case Study 5: Best Western

## Background

Best Western was created in 1946 to tap the boom in travel that followed the Second World War. Its founder, Meril K. Guertin, was a California motel owner who envisaged an association of independently owned and operated motels that would refer guests back and forth to each other. This concept came into being when Guertin visited several roadside hotels along the west coast and convinced them to join his consortium. Sixty-six properties contributed $10.00 each and began referring guests to one another. Only hotels that Guertin found to be of an acceptable standard in terms of quality and service could join, as 'travellers want clean rooms, good service and value for their dollar'.

In the late 1940s, the American middle class was finally enjoying easy access to both automobile ownership and vacations. Many young families began to travel extensively throughout the USA, staying in roadside motels along their route. Best Western started as a relatively informal link, with members making reservations for their clients next night's accommodation at a suitable affiliated property using collect phone calls between front desk personnel. During its initial years, Best Western restricted its operations to west of the Mississippi River, referencing properties along the main highways of the west coast of the USA. Later, it spread eastwards, engulfing Great Eastern and then expanding internationally. Today over 3700 properties fly the Best Western flag in over 70 countries and the company lodges over 40 million guests per year. However, Best Western is not a hotel company in the traditional sense. Instead it is a non-profit-making association of independently owned and operated hotels. This allows member properties to gain the benefits of being part of a large group, while at the same time allowing them to have their own individuality and personality. This philosophy is well illustrated by one of its advertising slogans: 'Best Western – A charming alternative to uniformity'. For the guest, Best Western signifies a carefully selected range of 3-star, 4-star and 4-star deluxe hotels, each of which is different and has retained its regional character, but which meets the stringent standards required for membership of the brand. It is this paradoxical combination of diversity and consistency that has made Best Western one of the best known and most trusted brand names in the world.

Best Western defines its mission as being to serve its members – the individual properties scattered around the world. It does this by providing a comprehensive range of member services, including voice reservations, electronic distribution, sales and advertising, brand identity, quality assurance, customer service, and various educational and training services. All of these services are funded through fees and dues paid by the membership and are designed to increase the profitability of the member properties. Managing such a company is unique. Each member has one vote and thus has a voice in how the brand is presented. Thus, to be successful, the company has to constantly ensure that it is giving members the service they require.

### The Best Western Reservation System

Best Western has always been at the forefront of hospitality technology. While the referral system based on collect phone calls worked while the company was small, it quickly became both inefficient and expensive to operate as the network grew. Like many others, the company turned to computerization to help increase communications and manage reservations. Initially it outsourced the function to companies like American Express, but eventually developed its own system, known as STAR, which was launched in 1974.

The STAR system was based on mainframes using the airline control protocol (ACP) and was one of the most advanced of its time. The system was connected to the major GDSs and also acted as the engine behind a series of CROs (in Phoenix, Arizona; Dublin, Ireland; and Milan, Italy) that provided 24-hour voice reservation services for members. Larger properties were connected to the central system through STAR terminals, which allowed them to check availability and make bookings at other Best Western properties. Thus, such properties could make onward reservations for clients at other properties without having to use the telephone. Properties without terminals could still contact the other property directly or could telephone the CRO to refer a guest onwards.

The STAR terminal also allowed properties to manage their own allocations on the system by manually opening and closing rates depending on demand. Front desk personnel could also access the central system to download reservations. However, these could only be printed, and thus had to be manually transcribed into the property-level reservation system or property management system to give an overall picture of the reservations situation.

While quite basic and not very interactive, the STAR system was efficient and reliable. It gave small and independent hoteliers unparalleled exposure in the global marketplace at a relatively low cost was responsible for processing nearly 25% on average of the members' reservations. The system went through several 'evolutions', each of which added additional features. However, its mainframe hardware and archaic database architecture soon proved themselves unsuitable for further development. In order to maintain its competitive advantage, Best Western decided that the system should be redeveloped to take advantage of advances in CRS technology and to allow for further expansion in the future. International development has been a major focus of Best Western for more than two decades, and it plans to continue this in the future in an effort to have 4000 properties in 75 countries by year 2000. According to Rob Wilson, Vice President of North American development, the companies growth will be 'intentional and strategic'. In effect, the group has the luxury to choose the kinds of markets and properties it needs to add critical distribution while building business for all members.

### Redeveloping the CRS

During 1996, whilst celebrating its golden anniversary, Best Western launched a new CRS. This project was driven by a desire to take advantage of new developments in CRS technology, and also to ensure that Best Western could deliver a 'consistent level of service' as the number of member properties continued to grow. The new $15 million reservations system is known as LYNX. According to Mary Swenson, Vice President of Worldwide Reservations and Sales: 'First the name epitomises an animal that is flexible, quick and responsive, all the attributes that a technical solution should have. Second, it stands for our link to the outside world, to our customers and to our members.'

LYNX provides Best Western properties with single image inventory capabilities. This means that inventory and reservation data is stored in just one location at the central level, and everyone (the CRO, the GDSs and the PMSs) accesses and feeds off this one resource. This avoids the problems associated with the maintenance of multiple databases and helps to ensure consistency as customers calling a toll-free number, the travel agent, a GDS or even the hotel itself all get the same information on availability and rates. The system is based on clusters of Digital Alpha-servers running a 64-bit UNIX operating system and is capable of handling in excess of 2000 transactions per second. This gives an ability to offer sub-second responses to users, even during peak periods, and makes the system particularly attractive to travel agents.

Each property throughout the chain has been provided with a PC running Windows 95 and connected to the central LYNX system by high-speed communications links. Within the US, these run a new PMS software package known as NOVA, which was developed in conjunction with Micros-Fidelio and is integrated with the new central system. This allows members to manage their room inventory in the central database by manipulating room types, rates, packages and extra person charges. It allows daily rate adjustments, room sales order changes and allows inventory to be segmented and opened to all distribution channels, including GDS, Internet and to other properties. Arrival lists are downloaded directly from the central database. In addition, NOVA also performs normal PMS functions such as tracking room status, guest folio management and interfacing with various auxiliary systems. Properties in Europe are still running STAR III or STAR IV, and thus do not yet have access to the full capabilities of the system.

LYNX has improved Best Western's service to the travel trade by permitting the most efficient level of connectivity, known as 'seamless connectivity'. This circumvents the limited and inadequate database architectures of the GDS by allowing travel agents direct access to the hotel CRS database. Thus Best Western is free to make an infinite number of marketing programs available on its system, allowing properties to promote the special features of their operation or to develop innovative packages, all of which will be available to and bookable by travel agents around the world. In addition, each property can include detailed descriptive information about their facilities, services, nearby attractions and amenities, and booking policies, thus providing travel agents with valuable information and giving each hotel a further opportunity to market itself and attract travel agent bookings. Developing facilities such as these would be impossible for independent properties without Best Western.

The development of the new system has also had a positive effect on CRO operation. It provides reservation agents with more sales tools than ever before, such as area maps, property photos and specific property information. A process called 'geo-coding' allows LYNX to select properties based on proximity to convention centres, theme parks, attractions and landmarks, as well as other properties, and the system also provides directions to the property. These improved functions help Best Western to better match the right hotel to each customer's needs, and have also reduced the talk time for each call, permitting increased call handling capability. Furthermore, the system uses a Graphic User Interface, which is very user friendly and which has helped to reduce training times and costs for reservation agents.

LYNX also includes advanced guest history capabilities that will allow Best Western to make use of database marketing in the future. The system has the power to store millions of guest preferences at thousands of properties around the world. These customer databases and online guest history facilities allow individual hotels to apply frequent guest discounts and track customer preferences worldwide. Oracle 7 was chosen as the underlying database technology for the new system. The advantages of this product include its scalability, its open systems operability and its high-volume online transaction capability. The database structure has been designed with customer service and sales productivity as its primary focus, and all property- and product-related reservation information is consolidated into one database that can be accessed from any guest service provider. 'This provides member hotels with unparalleled power to target guest service globally'.

Best Western is convinced that the system will provide real business benefits by enabling an increase in hotel revenues while significantly reducing system-related overheads and support costs at both corporate and property level. This has already started to happen, with, for example, a reduction in information systems staff from 137 to 69 after the installation of the new system (thus resulting in a major cut in payroll expenses). Furthermore, since the implementation of the new system, Best Western has increased its number of reservations dramatically, and REVPAR (revenue per available room) has also increased. The service provided by properties should also become more guest orientated and customized as a result of the guest history feature in the CRS that gives Best Western the ability to track guest preferences around the world.

# Chapter 3

# Distributing Small Hotel and Tourism Enterprises Electronically

An often-quoted statistic is that in the USA, well over half of hotel reservations come in through a CRS, but that in Europe, the norm is less than 10%. Why is this so? One of the major reasons is the way in which the hotel industry outside the USA is structured. Branding (whether owned or managed) is much less common in Europe. For example, less than 30% of hotels in the UK are part of a chain, group or consortium (Coby, 1993). Similarly, in Ireland, over 75% of accommodation units are independent, a characteristic also shared by other major destinations such as France, Germany, Switzerland and Austria (Vlitos-Rowe, 1992). As we have seen, computerized systems have traditionally been used to distribute a homogeneous product. One airline seat or hired car is more or less the same as any other. Even with chain hotels, you can be relatively certain of the physical characteristics of the product you have booked. A room in any of the major hotel brands will have standardized facilities and amenities (for example, two double beds, an en suite bathroom, a telephone and a television). However, where there is no brand present, you can be less certain of what you are booking. Contrast the room described above with one in an independently owned Irish country house hotel or a room in a French chateau. There may only be one bed (but it could be a four-poster), there might not be any telephone or television and the bathroom might be down the hall. And the room right next to it might be completely different. The possibilities for variation are infinite. Indeed, many of these types of properties market themselves not on their similarities, but on their differences. In order to incorporate them on to a CRS, very comprehensive descriptions are needed, not only to explain the physical characteristics of the product, but also to try to give a sense of their intangible qualities to the prospective buyer (Sheldon, 1993a).

Another key difference between the US and Europe is in terms of property size. In the US, a small hotel is considered to be one with 70–150 bedrooms, while in Europe, such a property would be considered relatively large (Richards, 1992). The average hotel size in the UK is only 25 bedrooms, in Ireland over 75% of properties have less than 30 rooms, while in Switzerland more than 90% of hotels have 50 rooms or less (European Commission, 1993). This size characteristic is mirrored throughout the rest of the world, not only in relation to hotels but also to tourism enterprises in general. In fact, Sheldon (1997) estimates that 98% of tourism enterprises worldwide can be classified as small and medium-sized enterprises (SMEs). This size characteristic makes the use of electronic distribution more difficult for several reasons. Firstly, many SMEs are managed by their owners, and are typically characterized by a lack of both strategic vision and marketing expertise, as well as an inability to utilize managerial tools to help overcome their operational problems (Buhalis, 1996). Many such managers cannot see the potential of electronic distribution, as the majority of their existing business either books directly or comes through a few regular intermediaries. Much of their business comes from the domestic market which, in general, is not well serviced by the existing GDS- and CRS-based systems (Archdale, 1993). Smaller operations can also have unusual priorities. For example, Archdale has pointed out that many small hotels want to maintain complete control over their room inventory and are unwilling to sacrifice this autonomy, even though it might be more efficient to give an allocation to a CRS or a representative company. Similarly, other researchers have reported that some B&B operations are reluctant to take clients that have booked electronically, as they feel it necessary to evaluate the client through personal contact in order to eliminate any undesirable elements (Pringle, 1995).

A relationship has also been shown between size and the tendency to use computer systems (a necessary prerequisite for using GDS/CRS), with smaller operations being far less likely to use technology (Frew and Pringle, 1995). SMEs also have limited resources, not only in terms of finance, but also in terms of management and staff time, and using electronic channels is (correctly or incorrectly) perceived as being complicated and unwieldy.

Finally, the issue of cost cannot be ignored. Smaller operations are less likely on several fronts to be able to afford to use electronic channels. Even when the hardware and other systems costs are ignored, many CRSs and representative companies charge joining fees, periodic subscriptions or require minimum monthly sales volumes, which may be cost prohibitive for smaller operations (Sheldon, 1993b). Most SMEs sell a relatively low price/low margin product, and therefore any fixed transaction fees represent a higher proportion of revenue than is the case with their higher-priced, more business-focused, cousins. Additionally, most electronic channels (particularly those involving travel agents) necessitate the payment of commission(s). For example, many CRSs take a commission of 3–5% of the revenue gained from the booking in addition to the 8–10% due to travel agents. When these are allied with the costs of keeping data on the systems up to date, nearly a quarter of the revenue from the transaction can be eaten away, thus making electronic channels a very expensive channel of distribution for smaller operations (O'Connor and Frew, 1998).

As was discussed in previous chapters, electronic distribution is now essential for anyone wishing to sell their products through travel agencies. However, the latter are no longer the sole users of the GDS. Today, corporate travel departments, meeting planners and wholesalers join the more than 350,000 travel agents that have the capability to make a reservation through a GDS (Gilbert, 1996). As a result, smaller hotel groups and independent properties increasingly have to ensure their presence on such systems, despite the considerable costs and technical difficulties involved (McGuffie, 1994). The situation is best summed up by Poon who states that the use of electronic distribution channels will be critical to the survival of hotels, as without them hotels will not be able to sell their bed nights (Poon, 1993). Many small hotel groups and independents have recognized that their future is threatened by the spread of electronic distribution and are looking for new ways to meet this threat. Two solutions have already been discussed: joining marketing consortia or making use of a third-party representative company. However, such options are expensive and it is precisely those properties that are most under threat, SMEs, who are least likely to be able to afford to pursue such a strategy.

## 3.1 Business vs. Leisure Travel

A close look at the hotels traditionally featured on GDSs/CRSs reveals something interesting: the type of accommodation featured is primarily focused on the business guest, irrespective of whether it is part of a hotel group or represented by a third-party company. This ties in well with the main market for the GDS: business travellers who use travel agents to plan their journey and make their reservations in advance (Emmer *et al.*, 1993). However, it ignores the other major component of the travel market, the leisure traveller, which is forecast to become increasingly important in the future (French, 1994).

The leisure segment has very different information needs to those of the business traveller. For example, most business travellers look on hotels as a place to stay; a necessary adjunct to the need to be in a certain place at a certain time (Richards, 1992). However, when travelling for leisure purposes, the same guest will be far more selective, and often will want to know more about the hotel (its location, its facilities, the local shopping and restaurants, and so on) before making a decision to stay there (Vlitros-Rowe, 1992). Traditional methods of electronic distribution, with their limited database structure and poor facilities for differentiation, make it difficult for travel agents to provide such information without contacting the property directly. Leisure travellers also tend to purchase a broader range of products when organizing a trip. In addition to transportation and accommodation, they also want information about (and to be able to book) entertainment and attractions, restaurants and bars and, increasingly, related products such as insurance, foreign currency, traveller's cheques and credit card services. While suppliers and intermediaries tend to think in terms of separate sectors (e.g. accommodation, transportation, etc.), the leisure traveller does not experience their visit in this way and is thus seeking more information on the 'total experience' (Pollock, 1992). To the customer, the perceived bundle of experiences of a whole destination has become far more important than any single component (WTO, 1997a).

The nature of the leisure sector itself is changing, with a gradual move away from tour operator-organized packages towards more independent travel (WTO, 1991). Travel agents are not well placed to meet the new demands of this trend: their margins are already low and they cannot afford to employ staff capable of providing the detailed authoritative advice on routes and destinations needed by these new independent travellers (Connell, 1996). In any case, this new breed of leisure tourist is less likely to make use of a travel agent, preferring instead to organize most elements of the trip for themselves (Poon, 1994). As a result, there is a demand for easily accessible tourist information, both before and during a trip, and particularly on SMEs such as hotels, guest houses and self-catering units, which have local character and flavour and thus are more attractive to the leisure guest than large multinational hotel chain properties (Buhalis, 1996). Those most effective in getting the required information to the potential tourist at the right stage of their decision-making process will have a major competitive advantage over their rivals (Sussmann and Baker, 1996).

As well as requiring information to help in their decision-making process pre-trip, the leisure traveller also requires information during their visit. This is particularly true as leisure travel moves away from pre-organized package tours towards more independent travel. Because people are travelling more flexibly and spontaneously, many purchase decisions are postponed until after arrival at the destination. For example, event, attraction and restaurant choices, and increasingly even accommodation reservations, are often not made until the guest is actually on location. Therefore the availability of high-quality, accurate and up-to-date tourism information within the destination is very important in helping to satisfy visitors' needs (Sheldon, 1993a). Sometimes the ability to make reservations is also required (for example, restaurant bookings or to reserve theatre tickets), while at other times, information provision on its own is adequate (for example, to help the guest establish the opening hours of local heritage attractions). These functions (providing tourist information both before and during the trip, and acting as a booking agent) are seen as being critical to the success of tourism in a region. For that reason, the role has traditionally been supported by national tourist authorities through their network of regional tourist organizations (RTOs) and tourism information centres (TICs).

## 3.2 The Role of Regional Tourism Organizations

Even though the majority of tourism enterprises are small, collectively they are very important to the economies of many regions. For example, tourism is Ireland's third largest export, a significant generator of foreign currency and one of the country's largest employers. SMEs tend to retain more of the flavour of the locality than their 'branded' competitors, and in many cases are the building blocks of the attractiveness of a city, region or country that attracts domestic or foreign tourists in the first place (Bordat, 1995). However, SMEs are particularly weak in terms of marketing knowledge and ability. Not only are they unaware of the techniques and tools available, but their efforts tend to be uncoordinated, inconsistent and ill-targeted, resulting in low effectiveness. The private sector, unaided, often under-provides resources for marketing the destination as the benefits from attracting an additional customer rarely go entirely back to the promoter, since a host of related ancillary services (e.g. transportation, excursions and retailing) benefit for free from the marketing expenditure (Baker *et al.*, 1996). Because of the importance of tourism revenues to both the economy and regional development, many governments feel it necessary to help tourism SMEs to actively promote both themselves and their region. This is usually achieved through the public funding of RTOs, which have as their mandate the promotion of a distinct geographical region. Marketing in this way is more effective than the efforts of individual suppliers, as people are not attracted to a region by the facilities on which, it turns out, they spend the most money – accommodation and eating. They come to enjoy other attractions, but they have to eat and sleep somewhere!

RTOs operate at various levels, from community to national or even transnational, and help to promote a region in several ways. Prior to the trip, they act as a central source of information, mailing brochures and responding to mail and phone enquiries. They actively promote the region at tourism exhibitions/travel shows and often maintain marketing offices in their major foreign markets to distribute information to potential visitors (Sheldon, 1993b). During the trip, RTOs help to provide information through a network of TICs where visitors can make enquiries and pick up brochures over the counter. Some of these offices also make reservations with hotels or other suppliers, sometimes for free or (more likely) for a fee or commission. This reservation processing function is important as it is generally accepted that the consumer wants more than just information when he contacts a tourist board. Inevitably, his ultimate aim is to make a booking, and the easier it is to find information, check availability and complete the booking, the more likely visitors are to both initially choose the destination and subsequently be satisfied with their experience (Sheldon, 1997).

However, providing such information and reservation services is problematic. Tourism is probably the ultimate dispersed industry. Tourists, whether business or leisure, come from everywhere and go everywhere, which means that everyone has unique information requirements. Even for the same room on 2 different days, there may be quite different information requirements. With tens of thousands of small heterogeneous suppliers and millions of individualistic purchasers, the permutations of information expand to a fearsome level. As we have already seem, GDS and CRS, with their primarily business client/travel agent focus are not capable of servicing this very complex and demanding mix of needs. A different type of distribution system, adapted to the needs of smaller, more leisure-focused, suppliers, is needed.

## 3.3 Destination Management Systems

This need has led to the development of a new kind of distribution system focused specifically on the requirements of both the RTOs and the smaller tourism supplier. These systems are known by a variety of different names, including, amongst many others, destination database systems (DDS), destination management systems, destination marketing systems (DMS), destination information systems (DIS), visitor servicing systems, travel information systems (TrIS) and central reservation and information systems (CRIS). Although their precise content varies, they all share a common philosophy – they have been designed to distribute information about a diverse and comprehensive range of tourism-related products, usually from a distinct geographical region, in an attempt to facilitate the highest economic use of the region's facilities (French, 1994). As a result, they are more inclined to include smaller establishments and non-accommodation tourism suppliers instead of just the major hotel chains. In most cases, their development has been driven by the RTOs, and thus their focus tends to be leisure-travel rather than business-travel based.

Being relatively new, DMS are still in a state of evolution and a universally accepted definition of a DMS is hard to come by as different countries and developers have different ideas as to what features should be offered. However, analysis of existing DMS reveals that several distinct categories can be identified as described in the following sections.

### 3.3.1 Information Only

The most basic form of DMS is one that stores and distributes information about the tourism suppliers, visitor attractions and events in a particular region (Crichton and Edgar, 1995). Such systems have their origins in the product database constructed by the tourist boards to help administer their region. These were usually developed for internal purposes, such as, for example, publishing guides or to assist in the registering, classifying or monitoring of premises (Archdale, 1993). By enhancing the database content to include additional descriptive data and incorporating information on attractions and events, tourist boards were able to create a valuable resource that could be used to help satisfy the tourist's need for information (Jones, 1992). Sheldon provides a comprehensive analysis of the data that should be provided by such systems:

> RTOs try to provide information on both private and public facilities. For the private sector, this includes information on accommodation (types, classifications, locations, rates, facilities and availability), transportation (modes, schedules, destinations, prices and availability), tours (components, sightseeing, activities, dates and availability), attractions, events and entertainment (descriptions, locations, prices, opening hours and availability) and restaurants (type of cuisine, location, size, price range and hours of opening). For the public sector, information should be included on parks, museums, galleries (opening hours, descriptions, entrance fees, locations and maps), public transportation (schedules, destinations, modes and prices), environmental (traffic conditions, weather reports, ski conditions or beach conditions) and legal requirements (border controls and health requirements).
> (Sheldon, 1996)

The information can be broken down into two distinct categories: (i) editorial content; and (ii) more specific data on individual products, services and providers. The background information (such as data about culture, places, history and landscape) helps to entice and inform the potential guest. It needs a high level of multimedia to be presented effectively, and thus should include photographs, video, film footage and sound clips. Once compiled, it has low 'volatility' and thus does not need to be updated often. Comprehensive data on tourism suppliers, attractions, activities, events, local festivities, available facilities and amenities as well as transportation/accessibility options to and within the destination must also be provided. This type of data has a higher volatility and must be recompiled and updated regularly to help ensure accuracy (Pollock, 1997a). Naturally, compiling, storing, managing and utilizing such a vast and complex range of data is very difficult. The potential therefore exists to use the power, accuracy and memory characteristics of computers to better manage this information. Once the tourist information is in digital format, it can be manipulated easily, reorganized at will, reused as often as required and communicated at electronic speeds (Pollock, 1997b).

Many RTOs make such databases available via computer systems to their counter staff in TICs. Such systems, often referred to as destination information systems (DIS) because they contain information on all suppliers and facilities in a destination, allow staff to respond quickly and efficiently to customer queries. For example, if a visitor is searching for a luxury hotel room by the beach, with TV and baby-sitting facilities at a cost of $100 per night, a query can be entered into the system, the database searched and a list of the resulting set of suitable properties printed for the customer. DIS improve this type of travel counselling by ensuring that all tourism products are presented to the customer (not just relying on the memory of the counsellor) and by assisting the counsellor in structuring the traveller's request. It thereby reduces the time and cost spent on each request and, at the same time, increases the quality of service provided.

The next logical step is to make this information available to the traditional travel intermediaries (tour operators and travel agents) to help service visitor information needs before arrival at the destination. In some cases, this has been achieved by loading the database on to the major GDS, which benefits both parties (Haines, 1993). Destination information is distributed to GDS users worldwide, thus greatly increasing the visibility of the region in the global marketplace (Buhalis and Main, 1996). The range of services available on the GDS is also enhanced, particularly in relation to the developing leisure market. Access to information of this type has become increasingly important to travel agents as their role changes from selling predefined package tours towards that of personal tour operator – packaging and consolidating different tourism goods and services together to meet the individual needs of their clients (Vlitos-Rowe, 1992). They need to be able to answer questions from their clients about a wide variety of topics, and thus access to the DIS should prove an invaluable asset as a source of accurate, reliable and up-to-date information. However, loading and maintaining such large amounts of data can be time-consuming, expensive and problematic for an RTO. A more effective solution is to electronically link the destination database to the GDS, in effect using the GDS as a communications network between the database and its users – the travel agents.

Another enhancement being implemented by several tourist boards is making the database directly available to the travelling public. As we will see in later chapters, attempts are being made to distribute data directly to potential visitors using CD-ROMs, teletext and over the World Wide Web. Within the destination, tourists can often access information on the region's facilities and attractions using multimedia touch screen kiosks located in public places such as shopping centres, airports and hotel lobbies.

One of the key benefits of using a destination database is that the information needed to service all of these information and distribution systems only has to be collected once. Traditionally, tourism suppliers have had to provide the same information to different distribution channels – for their individual brochures, for regional guidebooks, for tour operator catalogues and for electronic sources such as GDS, CRS and DMS databases or developing distribution channels such as CD-ROM guides or the World Wide Web. As the number of uses for the information increased, the amount of time that it took to manage it and the potential for errors similarly increased. With a destination database, information only has to be provided to and maintained in one location (Fig. 3.1). Since it is in electronic format, it can be copied easily and used for a variety of purposes (Pollock, 1997a). Similarly, users of tourism information – be they guide book producers or travel writers – have access to a single, accurate, multifunctional and digital source of information to help them produce appropriate promotional material.

### 3.3.2 Information and Reservations

For many RTOs, the creation of a 'destination database' is as far as it goes because they do not have the mandate to engage in commercial operations by selling products or they do not wish to compete with in-bound tour operators and their domestic travel agent community (Pollock, 1995a). However, simply providing information on its own is not very effective as a distribution strategy. As we have seen, customers searching for tourist information ultimately want to make a booking with as little trouble as possible. Therefore a DMS should help to facilitate this process. A logical extension of the DMS concept is thus to include booking facilities so that potential customers (whether pre-trip or post-arrival) can find the tourism product that

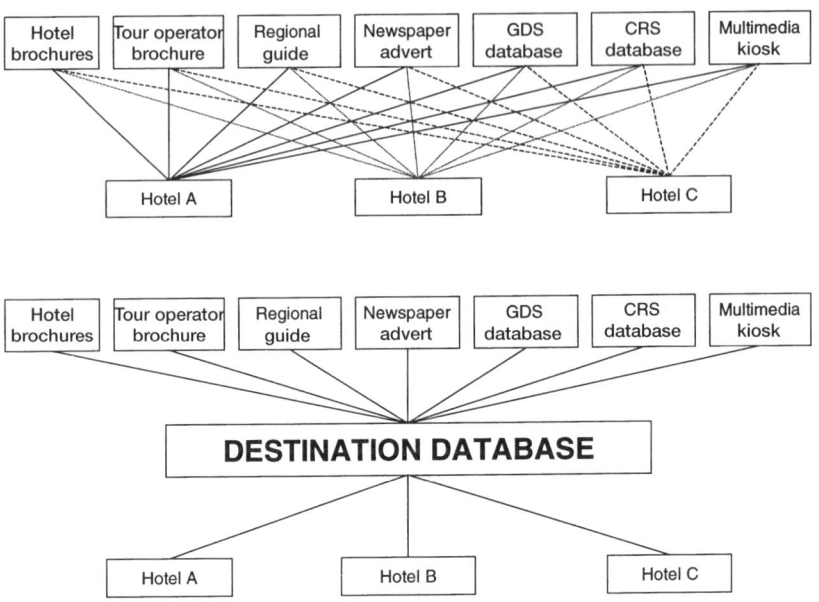

**Fig. 3.1.** Using a destination database to disseminate information.

meets their needs, check availability/rates and then make a booking in one seamless process. This increases both efficiency and customer service by changing the focus of the system from a simple electronic brochure into something significantly more powerful (Sussmann and Baker, 1996).

The development of the reservations function on DMS seems to follow a distinct pattern. Firstly the system is used as an internal booking system for the TICs – processing reservations for those clients already at the destination and generating revenue from fees and commissions which can be used to offset the development costs. As the system proves itself, its capabilities are expanded by the introduction of a telesales centre (sometimes by the RTO itself or sometimes in partnership with private enterprise), that helps to provide information and process bookings for those considering visiting the region. In both of these cases, a salesperson interrogates the database and processes the booking on behalf of the client, but it would obviously be more efficient to allow direct access to the system. For that reason, the next step is usually to make the reservations facility available to travel intermediaries over Videotext or the GDS and, ultimately, to bypass these intermediaries by distributing directly to the consumer over the World Wide Web, multimedia self-service kiosks or other direct channels (Jones, 1992).

Allowing the DMS to accept bookings brings several advantages to the RTO. Apart from the immediate revenue from fees or commissions (and thus changing the system from being a cost overhead into a revenue generator), being able to book electronically gives TICs many of the benefits which travel agents experienced when they first started using electronic booking systems. These include reduced costs, faster response times, improved customer service, increased control and reduced administrative work. SMEs, who receive a surprisingly high percentage of their bookings (12.5%) through referrals from TICs are easier to service and the effectiveness of the RTO/TIC network is easier to quantify, as the computerized system can produce statistics such as the number of enquiries processed, percentage of conversions and the value of the bookings processed.

However, incorporating reservations functions into a DMS is not without problems. SMEs, in particular, can be difficult to incorporate into the system as they have few common sales procedures, regulations or payments systems, and because of their aforementioned reluctance to give allocations (Archdale, 1993). Where the DMS is being used as a booking medium after the visitor's arrival at the destination, reservation lead times are short (often for later that same day) and therefore an effective method must be found to immediately communicate the reservation to the tourism supplier in real time. Lastly, as the transaction values of the goods/services being booked are low, it can be difficult to encourage commercial intermediaries (such as travel agents or tour operators) to book such facilities over the system as their resulting commission is consequently very small.

### 3.3.3 Information, Reservations and Client Databases

As we have seen, RTOs are primarily in the 'information brokerage' business; they use information as an operational and management tool to assist them in their role as intermediaries between tourism suppliers and consumers (Pollock, 1997b). The above discussion has focused on how data on producers, products and places are collected and distributed to consumers through the DMS. However, there is also a need for information to flow in the opposite direction. To operate effectively, tourism suppliers increasingly need to know more about their customers and their agents.

Mass marketing techniques, which focus on breaking up consumers into segments by grouping individuals with similar profiles together and treating them as if they were identical, has to a large extent become outdated (Jones, 1993). There are a variety of reasons for this, including the difficulty in measuring the results of marketing campaigns, and the waste of resources involved in promoting to a largely indifferent public. We now live in what John Naisbitt and other futurists have called *the age of the individual*. More and more customers are turning their backs on commodities (such as standardized travel packages), and demanding meaningful experiences that are personal and subjective and, if not unique, then at least tailor-made, flexible and professionally designed (Pollock, 1995a). To service their needs, marketers have to utilize targeted marketing which is firmly focused on the individual. Such direct or relationship marketing is based on certain theories, such as that past consumer behaviour is the best predictor of future behaviour and that customers are likely to share certain characteristics. It improves marketing productivity by allowing expenditure to be linked to results (as a direct campaign can be assessed by, for example, the number of resulting bookings), and by allowing market niches which are too small to be serviced by mass marketing to be profitably identified and targeted. In order to achieve this, 'a profound understanding of the complex requirements, expectations and desires of consumers, as well as their time and budget constraints, is vital' (Poon, 1989).

The value of storing and analysing customer information has traditionally been recognized by the hotel sector. Many hotel companies have devoted considerable resources to building and maintaining comprehensive guest history systems which track information about their guests. As the potential also exists for destinations to exploit this opportunity, several DMS have enhanced their facilities by incorporating client databases which store the demographic details, preferences and other information about visitors and potential visitors. This forms a valuable resource which can be used to more precisely identify and target potential customers, thus helping to reduce marketing costs and increase marketing effectiveness (Francese and Renaghan, 1990). By incorporating a suitable querying interface, these data can be used by members to perform very precise mail shots, telesales or other forms of direct marketing. In this way, marketing expenditure is reduced while at the same time effectiveness is increased as efforts are concentrated on a relatively interested audience (Sheldon, 1997). The data themselves can be compiled from a variety of sources. In addition to details of previous visitors, potential customer details can be collected from telephone or mail enquiries, from brochure requests or responses to advertising and promotions (Haines, 1993). This can be further supplemented by data purchased from or shared with third parties (such as hotel companies or other destinations) of individuals which have similar travel habits and psychographic characteristics to existing customers. The databases can also be used to provide valuable summary information about enquiry and visitor numbers, typical spending patterns, socio-economic classifications, etc., which can be useful in market and demand planning.

Further developments are possible. The rapid development in computer technology that has occurred over the past decade has greatly increased the potential of databases as sales and marketing tools. Storage costs have fallen to a level that encourages the collection and storage of far more data (such as individual purchase transactions) about each subject than was possible in the past; a phenomenon known as *data warehousing.* Destination-based loyalty/affinity schemes, based on smart card technology, have been proposed as a method of helping to collect and maintain such data (Main and O'Connor, 1998). *Data mining* techniques, coupled with the increased amount of processing power commonly available on the desktop, allow users to more thoroughly sift through and analyse such data to find exactly the potential clients which meet their required profile. Such analysis could greatly increase marketing effectiveness by providing valuable ammunition for advanced techniques such as psychographic analysis and lifestyle marketing.

### 3.3.4 Strategically Focused Systems

Most of the enhancements discussed above improve efficiency by adding to the functionality of the DMS. Another, more dramatic change has been proposed by various authors (most notably Buhalis, 1997, and Pollock, 1997a) which would change the scope of the system from one which is purely operational into one with a more strategic focus (Fig. 3.2).

As we have seen, DMS exist which provide information distribution, reservation processing and database marketing resources to the

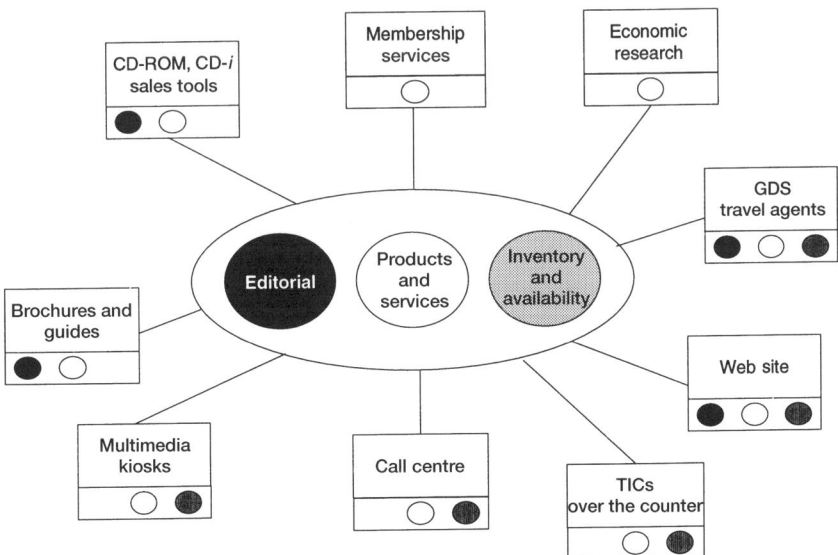

**Fig. 3.2.** The role of the DMS in destination management. Source: Pollock (1997d).

RTO and its member suppliers. However, most RTOs are not solely concerned with visitor servicing, most also have marketing, planning, development and industry support functions (Pollock, 1997b). In theory, a properly designed DMS should help to manage not just the marketing/promotion functions, but should transcend departmental and organizational boundaries to help manage the destination as a whole – a development which Buhalis has entitled DICIRMS (destination integrated computer information reservation management systems) (Buhalis, 1997).

Cooperating to manage the destination as a whole brings several advantages. For example, it has been shown that there is a high correlation between the competitiveness and profitability of SMEs and that of the destination in which they are located. After all, it is the amalgamation of all the different tourism goods, services and attractions in a particular location that is responsible for both attracting visitors in the first place and satisfying them during their visit. Thus, logic dictates that SMEs should concentrate on cooperating at a destination level to try to increase the competitiveness of the destination as a whole in order to increase their individual profitability (Bloch *et al.*, 1996b). In this way, they could increase the 'size of the pie', thus ensuring a bigger slice for each individual. Cooperation would also help to overcome the 'expertise' problems noted earlier. SMEs, being mainly family businesses, often employ family members who lack appropriate skills. Size constraints and seasonality also have an effect, as the SMEs cannot afford to overcome their knowledge/skills weaknesses by hiring appropriate professionals, offering competitive salaries or availing of appropriate training. Cooperation would allow them to improve their performance by pooling their resources and hiring expertise in strategic planning, financial planning, marketing, human resources and information technology, who could work for the benefit of the destination as a whole.

Of course a computerized system is not needed for such cooperation to occur. However, it could act as an enabling mechanism – facilitating interaction and communication between the SMEs – and could be used to help ensure the participation of the entire community in the project. Traditional community-based marketing mechanisms fail to spread the costs of a collective promotion of an area fairly. If half of the tourism suppliers in an area participate in a promotional campaign, there is no way to exclude the non-participating ones from benefiting from the additional business which the campaign generates. If, however, the DMS was used as both the information distribution tool and the reservations engine, only those who support the DMS would get bookings, thus reducing the problem. Such a system would also help to manage supply by permitting the real-time collection of availability data, in effect allowing yield management to be performed at the destination level. The DMS could also take on a tour operator role by helping individuals to combine a variety of different tourism services (including incoming transportation, transfers, accommodation and visits to attractions) together into self-customized packages. By facilitating 'diagonal integration', the system would allow suppliers at different levels of the distribution chain to work closely together and mutually reinforce each other (Poon, 1993). This would facilitate the production and distribution of 'clusters of interrelated services' (which need not all be tourism specific). Such products would directly service the new leisure clientele, which would welcome the facility to design their own flexible, tailor-made and integrated package that could be seamlessly booked at the touch of a single button.

The enhanced communications would facilitate closer cooperation between tourism suppliers and help to overcome some of the diseconomies of scale associated with being a small business. For example, Buhalis has also suggested that such a communications network could provide additional facilities and services to SMEs. These could include:

- *tele-banking*, which would help reduce banking costs and speed up the processing of credit card transactions;
- *tele-training*, which would allow video-conference style training of line staff to be carried out, particularly during the off season when both the personnel and the DMS would be under-utilized; or even
- *tele-consulting*, which would allow remotely located SMEs to make use of specialist consultants who could advise and assist over the system (Buhalis, 1997).

Similarly, the communications system could be used to develop a centralized purchasing facility. Orders for raw materials could be automatically collected and amalgamated on a daily or weekly basis. In this way, more favourable prices could be negotiated with suppliers because of the larger volumes involved.

Increased inter-connectivity could also be used to help collect and disseminate tourism statistics. Such information is important in measuring the performance of the destination and as a means of spotting trends, but currently suffers from the difficulty in collecting and analysing it in a time-frame where it is still relevant. In many cases, such information is not published until 2–3 years after its collection, and thus its usefulness in decision-making is limited. In the past, the lack of an appropriate technology to interconnect all the suppliers made these tasks difficult, but recent advances mean that the problem is no longer technological but organizational – putting in place systems and procedures to facilitate the process (Pollock, 1997a). A DICIRMS could help to solve this problem by seamlessly collecting, compiling and analysing relevant data automatically. The same communication medium could then be used to share such information and market intelligence with individual tourism suppliers, along with information about the operations, assistance schemes and promotions of the RTO. In this way, suppliers would be more aware of the activities and efforts of the destination as a whole, which would help to further enhance the feeling of cooperation.

Unfortunately, DICIRMS are currently just a theoretical concept. While some of the elements discussed above are starting to be implemented in some systems, there is no operational DMS that provides such a comprehensive and integrated service to its members. One issue is clear: DMS cannot provide competitive advantage in the long term. Because of their obvious potential in terms of operational efficiency, promotion and regional development, most destinations will eventually use such systems in one form or another. Therefore continuous innovation will be necessary to keep one step ahead of the competition (Buhalis, 1997).

## 3.4 Key Success Factors

Buhalis has estimated that more than 200 destination-orientated systems of various kinds have emerged over the past few years (Buhalis, 1997). Despite their potential, few DMS have outlived their pilot and development stages to evolve into fully fledged, fully operational systems. While an in-depth analysis of the reasons for this are beyond the scope of this text, a review of the literature on these systems and on DMS in general reveals several key factors which are essential for the successful development of a DMS. Some of these are described in the following sections.

### 3.4.1 Public and Private Sector Support

There has been considerable debate as to how a DMS project should be initiated, set up and managed. Many authors feel that the involvement of the public sector, in particular the RTO, is essential for several reasons. Firstly, there is an obvious overlap between the marketing, promotion and management functions of the RTO and the capabilities of a well-designed DMS and thus cooperation seems logical. Secondly, given the high development costs and the limited potential for adequate returns in the initial years of operation while booking volumes are still low, financial support from the public sector is essential in the start-up phase (Haines, 1993). As will be discussed below, RTO involvement also helps to ensure the accuracy, fairness and completeness of the supplier data; and, lastly, it has been shown that to be successful, a DMS must be integrated into the overall marketing and promotion strategy of the destination (Buhalis and Cooper, 1992). This can only occur where the RTO is actively involved in the design and operation of the system.

There are, of course, arguments against public sector involvement. From a market perspective, it can be argued that DMS with RTO involvement would act as a publicly subsidized competitor to travel agents, CRSs and hotel booking agents (all of whom earn revenue by making reservations for clients) and, as such, DMS would be an unfair form of competition. It has also been pointed out that a government agency structure is not suitable for a system of this type. For example, French (1994) argues that while governments and RTOs should help to define the vision and scope of such projects, they should be implemented by the private sector, as government organizations are too politicized and bureaucratic to successfully operate such a system. In particular, he cites their rigidity as being the factor that prevents them from responding quickly and decisively to opportunities. He stresses that DMS must operate as commercial enterprises; with quantified performance measures, full accountability, a streamlined organizational structure which facilitates responsiveness and innovation, and motivated, empowered staff with the authority to take advantage of opportunities as they develop (French, 1994). Only a private sector organization is likely to have such a structure.

At the same time, a purely private sector-operated DMS is unlikely to be successful, as its requirement to make profits would have an effect on its methods of operation. Even if the seemingly insurmountable issues of finance and return on investment are ignored, a commercial organization could not be expected to list, promote or distribute those establishments which resulted in greater costs than the revenue they generate. The technical and contractual challenges presented by SMEs, taken together with their small booking volumes and low transaction value, would mean that many such establishments would have to be excluded, thus affecting the comprehensiveness of the system (Hurst, 1992). In addition, many users would question the objectivity of a commercial DMS, in a manner similar to the ongoing debate that rages over the impartiality of hotel and restaurant guide books today. The question would always be asked: is a particular establishment getting priority because it is the one which best meets the client's needs, or it is because it paid the highest fees to the commercially operated DMS? (Baker *et al.*, 1996).

The most acceptable solution would seem to be a compromise – that the project should be public sector-led and -financed in the initial stages, and that the roles should reverse and the private sector should take control once the system is operational. At this stage, the RTO should maintain a minority interest to help ensure completeness, accuracy and objectivity and to protect the interests of both consumers and smaller principals, while the day-to-day operation and management of the system should be the responsibility of the private sector partner. Perhaps this function should be offered for competitive tender periodically to help ensure that only the most efficient, commercially orientated company is involved in its operation.

### 3.4.2 Data Quality

Most authors agree that one of the most important factors in ensuring the success of a DMS is the quality of the data it contains. Firstly, such data have to be accurate. False or misleading information leads to mismatched expectations, and therefore to customer dissatisfaction, and damages the credibility of the system as a whole. Secondly, the data must be kept up to date, which can be a major challenge given that tourism-related data are so time sensitive and perishable. Rates, schedules, events and opening hours change with the day, week, month and season. Thirdly, the data must be comprehensive. A DMS that lists 10 hotels in a resort that has several hundred is of limited value. One that contains data on accommodation only is of less value than one which covers the entire spectrum of tourism information (Milchem, 1997). As a result, the DMS must contain details about all of the establishments, attractions and events of interest to visitors to the particular destination. It should not limit itself to individual products, but should also list and distribute the packages created by tour operators or other intermediaries. Failure to include such products would jeopardize confidence that the DMS can provide the best available deal (Buhalis, 1997).

In short, the system should be perceived by the user to be the most accurate, timely and complete source of information available about the region. Thus, quality control of the data, though difficult to achieve, is vitally important. While penalties for misrepresentation may discourage the casual offender, this may not be enough. An alternative strategy would be to link the listing on the DMS to the regulatory and grading functions of the RTO. This would help to ensure completeness, as all registered operations would be included, and also ensure accuracy, as descriptions, facilities and amenities could be audited as part of the grading process.

### 3.4.3 Technology

Given the importance of keeping the information in the database accurate and up to date, an appropriate form of communication between the supplier and the DMS is needed. Information also has to be able to pass in the opposite direction quickly and easily, as reservations often occur very close to their time of use and the supplier must be alerted to them.

In the past, the postal system was used to both collect information using periodic questionnaires and forms, and also to inform suppliers of upcoming reservations. Obviously such a system was too slow and did not permit frequent updates. Communication by telephone overcame these difficulties, but is very labour intensive (for both the DMS and the suppliers) and also results in high communications costs. The ideal solution would be to have terminals or computers located in each suppliers, which they could use to access the system directly to update their data and to process reservations. Unfortunately, as was discussed at the beginning of the chapter, SMEs are the least likely to either be able to afford or be able to use such technology. Repeated research has shown the need for a solution to this problem, but no one to date has found an acceptable technology. Such a system would have to be cheap to purchase and operate, intuitive, idiot proof, have a good user interface, and need little special hardware or knowledge on the part of the user. Experiments with fax-based systems and computer-assisted telephony have failed to gain widespread acceptance. Perhaps the diffusion of Internet-based technologies (such as Network Computers, Browser Boxes, etc.) will prompt the development of a technology which can be used for this purpose.

### 3.4.4 The External Environment

The final factor that can be identified in ensuring the success of the DMS is the need to develop links between the system and the outside world. As we have seen, many DMS, particularly in their initial stages, focus on acting as an information and internal booking system for the TICs. While this helps to greatly increase the efficiency of the RTO, it is unlikely to generate sufficient booking volumes to either make the system self-sufficient or to prove its worth to suppliers and encourage them to think of it as a major channel of distribution.

Links with external systems, which help to distribute the DMS information to a wider audience and increase the volume of bookings flowing through the system are therefore important. Many DMS operators stress the importance of distributing through the traditional travel intermediaries (Vlitos-Rowe, 1992). Despite the growth in independent travel, tour operators and travel agents are still one of the most important channels of distribution. By providing access to the DMS database and reservations engine over videotext systems, through GDS gateways or over the World Wide Web, RTOs provide intermediaries with a powerful marketing and operational tool which make it easier for them to service their customers. Regions which provide such facilities will have competitive advantage in the short run, as they are more likely to be sold by intermediaries, thus increasing the all-important level of bookings flowing through the system.

Attempts are also being made to distribute directly to the customer over a variety of different routes, again with the aim of increasing booking volumes. In all cases the central source of tourism information, and the main engine for accepting, processing and booking reservations must be the DMS. It cannot operate in isolation, however, and thus must be referred to in all marketing and promotional materials, on print and broadcast advertisements, at trade shows and conventions. It must be thoroughly integrated into and be pivotal to the region's overall marketing strategy (Haines, 1993). In short, the DMS must become part of the brand identity of the region, so that when a customer thinks of the region, they automatically think of the DMS as the place to find information and book tourism products.

**Note**: for a more comprehensive discussion of the critical success factors in DMS implementation and operation, see Frew and O'Connor (1998) or Frew and O'Connor (1999).

# Case Study 6: Tyrol Information System

Tyrol Information System GmbH (hereafter referred to as TIS) is one of the leading examples of a DMS. Originally established at the beginning of the 1990s to help distribute information to regional tourist offices within the Tyrol, its capabilities have been expanded to encompass a wider variety of distribution channels but it has remained true to its information-only origins.

### System Background

When the system was conceived, tourism was a key industry in Austria. For example, total annual turnover for the leisure sector as a whole in 1990 came to about $25 billion. Foreign currency earnings from tourism came to $12 billion, which covered 70% of the country's trade deficit. The Tyrol was Austria's most important tourism region, generating more than 50% of foreign currency earnings, over 35% of the total bed nights and approximately 30% of gross regional product. However, the Tyrol also suffered greatly from seasonality, with over-capacity for most of the year, and under-capacity during the brief summer and winter seasons. The Tyrolean RTO, a publicly funded body charged with both the marketing and strategic development of tourism in the region, needed to find a way to expand demand, particularly during the low season.

Tourism officials noted the growing discrepancy between the highly professional international tourism suppliers with their sophisticated data processing and communications networks on the one hand, and the smaller local supplier community at the other end of the spectrum. Existing electronic distribution channels, such as the GDS, tended to only list products 'that could be sold without supplementary costs and, consequently, … because information gathering is expensive … they do not include everything the Tyrol has to offer' (Vlitos-Rowe, 1992). Market research revealed that consumers wanted information on prices, accommodation, resort accessibility and leisure amenities, but that these information needs were not being serviced adequately by the existing channels. The RTO felt that this was a limiting factor in the healthy development of tourism in the region, and thus, as a strategic move, decided to develop an alternative computerized information system, to be known as the Tyrol Information

This case study was prepared by Peter O'Connor, Assistant Professor, Institut de Management Hôtelier International (IMHI), as a basis for discussion rather than to illustrate either effective or ineffective handling of an administrative problem.
All rights reserved.

System, to help distribute information on smaller suppliers.

An important characteristic of TIS is that it was designed solely for information purposes and had no reservations functions. When developing the system, the Tourist Board saw its role as primarily an information conduit, gathering information about the local, regional and national tourist product and distributing it to potential customers, both locally and worldwide (Fig. 3.A). It saw itself as having a supporting function in promoting the tourism product but not in selling it. This was instead left to the individual suppliers or to incoming agents operating at the regional level. At the same time, the RTO also needed to disseminate information on current trends and the general market situation, and recognized the potential of the system for communication with both the local tourist boards and with tourism suppliers. Thus the initial system developed had two main functions: to make tourist information about the Tyrol more available in the marketplace and to facilitate communication between the RTO and local tourist boards/ suppliers.

The design of the system was greatly influenced by the structure of the tourist board. The Tyrolean RTO ('Tirol Werbung' in German) is composed of an affiliation of 254 local tourist boards. In effect, it

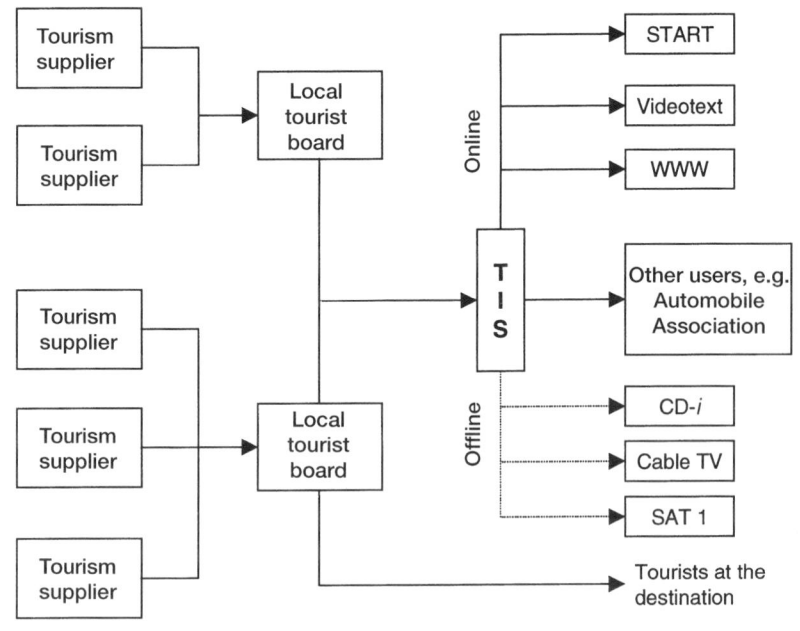

**Fig. 3.A.** Structure of the Tyrol Information System.

forms a large network, with the local boards all participating in the formulation of overall marketing strategy and policy. The RTO itself has no independent decision-making powers, which helps to ensure that the interests of the industry are always respected. TIS was designed to strengthen this structure by using a distributed data architecture. All data are stored locally, close to where they are most frequently used, which helps to reduce communications costs. However, each local board can also access the entire database. The central office operates as a communications server, consolidating the databases from each region and then distributing a copy of the overall database to each user. Updates take place daily so that any data in the system are at most 1 day old, which is more than adequate for purely informational purposes. A decentralized approach is also used for data collection. Each local board is responsible for keeping data on their region up to date on the system. Similarly, each local board is able to specify what data they want to receive from the central system so that resources are not wasted in downloading information that is never used.

### System Features

Conceptually, the system can be divided into two parts: a module designed to provide clients with information about the Tyrol; and a marketing/management module designed to disseminate statistical and other data to the local tourist boards and tourism suppliers.

- The *information module* is the main focus of the system, and contains data on a wide variety of tourism products and services, including accommodation, sports facilities, transportation information, events and special promotions. Data is maintained about over 43,000 tourism products or services including over 12,000 accommodation products. As there are only approximately 6000 hotels in the Tyrolean region, nearly 50% of the latter are small operations that would not otherwise be represented electronically. Real-time information on snow conditions, roads, traffic, water temperatures and glaciers is also maintained on the system, with the cooperation of the Meteorological Institute of Innsbruck and the Austrian Automobile Club.
- The *management information module* is smaller, but is critical to the acceptance of the system by the local tourist boards. Its content was based on a survey of the latter's information needs, and it provides information that is of interest to both the tourist boards and tourism suppliers. This includes: the region's marketing plan, information on trade fairs, press conferences and other promo-

tional activities, details of subsidies available for tourism development, and information on advertising publication schedules and prices. An organizational chart of the RTO is available on the system to help suppliers become familiar with the structure of the board and related organizations. Addresses of major players in the tourism industry (such as travel agencies, tour operators or the travel media) are also available and can be used for direct mail purposes. Lastly, market information and statistics on both source countries and competing destinations are provided and powerful decision-support tools are available to help users interpret this data.

Technically the system had to be designed to take existing legacy computer equipment into account and thus had to be platform independent. The central database is maintained on an IBM RS 6000 at the central office in Innsbruck, and communication is undertaken using modems and telephone lines. The system is written in a 4GL database language, and is independent of the operating system. Local offices use a mixture of MS-DOS, Unix, AIX and OS/2 based systems, although IBM-compatible PCs running under MS-DOS quickly emerged as the most common configuration. The user interface is menu driven, with shortcut keys for the more common functions – which is adequate given that the system is designed to be used by tourist office personnel. Training on both the use and the capabilities of the system is mandatory for all new local tourist board staff.

### The Current Situation

Over 100 local tourist offices currently use the TIS system, and collectively these represent more than 80% of the market. However, this success has not made the company complacent. From its inception, the development of TIS was seen as a continuous process and not just a single project. The developers see the system as a learning process, and are not afraid to experiment with new and developing technologies to get their tourist information to the marketplace. Therefore, although the system was originally designed to be used solely by tourist board staff, it has evolved and its distribution channels now include:

- START: TIS data is available over the START reservation system, a videotext-based system used by approximately 14,000 travel agents in German-speaking countries. Out of a total of 2000 pages of information about Austria in the START system, more than 50% deal with products in the Tyrol region and are provided by TIS.

- Videotext systems: the data contained in the TIS information module is available over a variety of videotext systems outside of Austria, including the German Dataex-J system and the French Minitel system. This allows millions of consumers (all within a day's drive of the Tyrol) to check snow and road conditions interactively on their terminals, and to request brochures or other forms of promotional material for products which interest them. This market is particularly important, as German tourists are more likely to plan their leisure time themselves rather than take a package tour. Despite the technical drawbacks of this type of system, it is being widely used. For example, during the height of the winter 1995 season, T-online was accessed 6500 times per day to find information about up-to-date conditions in the Tyrol.
- Other users: in addition to the local tourist boards, electronic access to the system has also been provided to certain other organizations, such as the Austrian Tourist Board in Vienna, the OAMTC and the ADAC (Austrian–German Automobile Associations).
- CD-*i*: taking advantage of developments in computing and multimedia, TIS experimented with the production of a CD-*i* (compact disk interactive)-based promotional tool. The disks incorporated an interactive show with combined text, photos, video clips, music and speech, thus giving the potential visitor a taste of the attractions of the region. TIS intended to use these disks at self-service kiosks at the destination, and also on promotional stands at travel exhibitions and shows. However, unlike its more popular cousin the CD-ROM, users need a special player to view CD-*i*-based media, and thus this channel never gained widespread acceptance as a distribution or entertainment medium, and the project was discontinued.
- Cable TV: in the Tyrol, more than 55,000 consumers can retrieve TIS tourist information through their cable television sets. This facility is aimed at local people rather than tourists, but the latter can similarly access the system through the television sets in their hotel rooms.
- World Wide Web: not surprisingly, TIS information is also available over the World Wide Web. In a separate development, a new service known as TISCover provides access to the TIS information to users all over the world. Several pages of texts and images about each hotel, along with a star rating as an indication of quality are maintained on the Web site, and further information can be requested by Email. Interestingly, replies to requests for further information are by telephone or fax, not by Email. However, this

appears to be an add-on service as the details of only 107 hotels were available on the site 6 months after its opening.

Each of these developments has made the information contained in TIS available to a wider audience. Given the trends towards more frequent and shorter holidays, consumers need access to accurate, comprehensive and up-to-date information about tourism products. By making it easy and convenient for consumers to access such information through the TIS system, the Tyrolean Tourist Board hopes to gain competitive advantage over other destinations.

### The Future

Given their culture of innovation, the TIS developers are continuing to develop and focus the system. For example, the company is, in conjunction with Siemens Nixdorf and START, developing a more powerful version of the system that will provide destination information, process reservations and provide back-office functions to the local tourist offices, all integrated into a single package. Discussions have also taken place between TIS and the Austrian Ministry of Economic Affairs to expand the system into a DMS for the entire country, thus making it the single source of information for Austrian tourism as a whole.

# Case Study 7: Gulliver

Ireland is an island nation, located on the north-west edge of Europe and its economy is highly dependent on tourism. For example, in 1995 4.2 million people visited Ireland, generating IR£1.5 billion in foreign earnings. Tourism formed 6.4% of GDP, and supported employment for 1 in every 13 Irish workers. Despite their collective importance, Irish tourism operations tend to be relatively small in comparison with their international counterparts (for example, over 85% of accommodation units in Ireland are SMEs with fewer than 30 rooms). Businesses tend to be owner-managed, are unlikely to be part of a chain or marketing consortium and are traditional and conservative in operation. As a result, individual properties tend to be very different, both in terms of style and facilities. In effect, their main selling point stems from the individuality of their product – uniqueness is their main attraction. These characteristics also make the Irish tourism product very difficult to include on electronic distribution systems. Furthermore, from a cost perspective, such properties often cannot justify the high levels of commission and fees charged by the traditional distribution systems.

Given its importance to the Irish economy, the government has in recent times placed increasing emphasis on tourism, and has focused this through the use of strategic plans aimed at increasing both tourist numbers and yield. For example, in 1987, the Irish government presented Bord Failte (the Irish Tourist Board) with the challenge of doubling Irish tourism within a 5-year period. The four-part strategy devised to achieve this involved developing and enhancing the Irish tourism product, promoting this product more aggressively, increasing its competitiveness internationally and distributing it more effectively. One of the key initiatives in this overall growth programme was the Gulliver project.

## Gulliver: the Initial System

Gulliver was developed as a joint venture between Bord Failte and the Northern Ireland Tourist Board (NITB). Its primary goal is to be 'the main channel of distribution for information and reservations on all major aspects of tourism in Ireland'. The objectives of the system are twofold: (i) to make it easier for a tourist to choose Ireland as a

This case study was prepared by Peter O'Connor, Assistant Professor, Institut de Management Hôtelier International (IMHI), as a basis for discussion rather than to illustrate either effective or ineffective handling of an administrative problem.
All rights reserved.

destination; and (ii) to improve visitor servicing while in Ireland. Rather than competing with other distribution systems (electronic or not), Gulliver sees itself as a facilitator, with its role being to define standards, remove communication barriers and reduce communication costs.

Funding for the project came from a variety of sources, including EU development grants (IR£2.9m), Bord Failte (IR£2.6m), International Fund for Ireland development grants (IR£1.6m) and the NITB (IR£1.5m). Development commenced in 1990, following a technical feasibility study. The initial system was designed to be both real time and online, and used dumb terminals connected via leased lines to minicomputers located in each of the RTO head offices. These were in turn connected via leased lines to a Digital VAX 6320, on which the Gulliver system and its databases resided. The other major technical element of the system was a Minitel Videotext service, which provided a low-cost method of allowing accommodation providers to keep their availability/prices dynamically updated on the system.

Gulliver's prime role was seen as being to facilitate the distribution of tourism products from the supplier to the customer by providing a flow of accurate, reliable and relevant information. The ultimate vision is that it would become the definitive repository of tourism information for all Ireland, north and south. Unlike existing electronic tourism distribution services, Gulliver was designed from the outset to be comprehensive in its supplier database. For example, basic details of all Tourist Board-approved properties were included on the system. However, its scope was not limited to accommodation alone. Details of entertainment (including a calendar of events), places to visit (ancient monuments, gardens, national parks, museums and art galleries), activities (such as facilities for angling, golf, sailing and walking), transportation (air and ferry schedules, train and bus timetables, car rental information) and other general tourism information (such as passport/visa requirements, health regulations and climatic conditions) were all included on the system. Reservation facilities were also provided. Tourism suppliers could give allocation of their product to the system, which was then available for sale electronically. Users could also make reservations with suppliers who chose not to give allocations by telephoning them directly to check availability and make the booking. In such cases, many of the benefits of using an electronic system in the first place were lost and thus preference was given to the former type of supplier.

From the point of view of the customer (be they an individual or a bulk purchaser such as a tour operator), Gulliver provides several key advantages. Users have direct and instant access to the vast database of tourist information discussed above, containing up-to-date information about tourism services, events, attractions, places of interest and, of course, comprehensive information on accommodation providers. Electronic search facilities assist them in quickly and easily finding exactly the information they require. Lastly, electronic booking facilities allow them to check availability and rates, make their booking(s) and immediately receive confirmation. All of this is achievable without the monetary and time costs associated with the traditional telephone/fax methods of searching for information and making reservations.

The initial service was piloted in early 1992 and, following the correction of some initial problems and incorporation of user feedback, went online in August of 1992. Although a variety of different distribution channels were eventually planned, the initial demand-side users of the system were the RTOs and the TICs located throughout Ireland which primarily service the tourist already in the country. A system to help service these facilities was essential for a number of reasons. The Irish tourism industry suffers from periods of localized peak demand, which is compounded by a lack of information. For example, tourists might be unable to find suitable accommodation in Tralee, while at the same time there might be an excess of supply in Killarney, just 20 miles away. The traditional source for such information is the aforementioned TICs. Prior to the introduction of Gulliver, staff in these centres had to rely on paper-based systems to deal with customer enquiries. By definition, these were expensive to maintain and difficult to keep up to date. Customer service representatives had to telephone each accommodation supplier directly to check availability, which was both time-consuming and expensive in terms of telephone charges. The TICs also had high labour costs, as it took considerable amounts of time to service each customer enquiry. Thus, overall, the manual system being used was very ineffective.

The development of Gulliver helped to ease many of these problems. The introduction of the computerized system allowed staff in the TIC to search for both information and availability on their terminals, and allowed them to more easily match customer requirements to appropriate suppliers because of the comprehensive database provided by the system. As a result, recommendations no longer needed to be limited to the individual knowledge of the staff member. The system was at its most effective where a supplier had given an allocation of their product to the system. In such a case, the entire booking, from the initial enquiry through the booking process and the payment of a deposit, could be completed on the system in a far shorter period of time than was possible with the previous manual system, thus leading to increased customer satisfaction. The operation of the TIC as a whole also benefited, as customer turnover was faster and labour/communication costs per booking were lower. Such benefits would have been further enhanced with the introduction of the planned self-service kiosks, which would have made the service available directly to the public 24 hours a day, 365 days a year with little or no transaction cost for the tourist board.

However, further deployment of the system was delayed when a system review in 1993 identified some fundamental problems with the technological strategy being used. For example, the use of a centralized real-time approach meant that extremely high levels of central computing power were required, which sometimes resulted in performance difficulties at peak times, particularly during the summer season. Similarly, the use of dedicated leased lines resulted in high telecommunications costs. The review concluded that, from a technological point of view, a centralized online system was not appropriate to achieve the objectives of the project. Another problem also became apparent at this time. Gulliver used a simple text-based interface for both its suppliers and its demand points, in part to minimize the amount of data being transmitted over the system. However, developments in technologies such as multimedia, CD-ROMs and the growing use of the graphic-rich World Wide Web made the Gulliver system look increasingly out of date. Given the marketing orientation of the system, the opportunity existed to provide a much richer user interface incorporating high-quality images, sound and even video, thus enhancing the effectiveness of Gulliver as a sales and marketing tool. The limitation, however, was that each of these enhancements has a requirement in terms of the volume of data which must be transmitted over the system. As the existing system was already overloaded at peak times, it was clear that it would not be capable of handling such an increased workload.

A different approach was clearly needed. Subsequent investigations into Gulliver's data storage patterns and access profiles revealed an interesting picture. The data stored could be clearly segregated into static and dynamic elements. Static data represented the vast majority (approximately 90%) of the database and described each supplier's products and services. These data rarely changed but were accessed a great deal. Dynamic data represented far less in terms of volume since they usually concerned availability and rates, but at the same time changed very frequently and thus needed to be kept up to date at all times. This was one of the most significant findings of the review and became one of the cornerstones of the new Gulliver system.

### Re-engineering the Gulliver System

In 1994, the decision was taken to re-engineer the Gulliver system, retaining the concept and vision but updating its technology. Instead of having a single central storage and processing resource, the new Gulliver system was redesigned as a distributed client-server system using state-of-the-art communications and computing technology. Static data are accessed locally on PCs located in the demand points, and users link to the central system only when they need access to dynamic data such as up-to-date availability and rate information. This distributed approach means that both central-processing requirements and communication costs are minimized.

The central system has been redesigned so that each transaction (such as, for example, bookings, cancellations, or changes in allocation and price) is processed using a series of electronic messages (in effect, a customized form of EDI) rather than through real-time online access. These electronic transactions are processed and a response transmitted, again using a predefined format, to the original remote computer. In operation, this means that the seller first searches through the static data stored on his local PC or local area network when looking for a suitable product for the customer. Once a suitable one has been identified and the customer wishes to make a booking, the local system automatically accesses the central system using a router and an ISDN line. A response time of less than 8 seconds is typical once the client is connected. Overall, this distributed approach is far more effective in terms of both costs and operating efficiency.

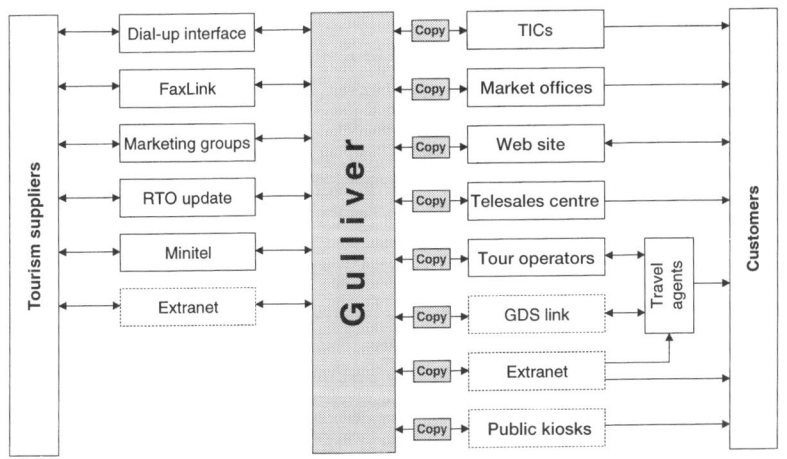

**Fig. 3.B.** The Gulliver system.

The key issue of how to allow tourism suppliers access to the system for availability update purposes was also addressed by the new system. The majority of Irish tourism enterprises are SMEs, and make little use of information technology. The initial Gulliver system incorporated a facility, based around the Minitel Videotext system, which allowed suppliers to connect to the system, check on reservations and update availability at a relatively low cost. However, the poor user interface and slow operating speed of this technology made it unpopular with the smaller operations, at which, ironically, it had been targeted. Cost was also a factor, and since many suppliers only used their system to communicate with Gulliver, the use of Minitel was perceived to be expensive in relation to the benefits gained. As a result, many smaller suppliers chose to simply communicate with Gulliver via telephone or fax, which was inefficient as it required manual data entry by the central staff to keep the information on Gulliver up to date.

The re-engineered system tried to reduce this problem in a variety of different ways. A PC-based solution was developed that allowed suppliers to dial in and use the electronic messaging standard to collect reservations/cancellations and change availability/rates. This could be run as a stand-alone program, or could be incorporated into third-party software, thus allowing it to link directly into hotel PMSs. Initial users included two large Irish marketing groups, representing over 2000 accommodation outlets, who successfully linked themselves to the Gulliver system using this messaging approach and manage allocations/reservations on behalf of their members. An alternative method was developed for use by suppliers with low levels of transactions, which was based on the use of a fax machine and pre-printed fax forms. The barcoded forms are sent to the central system from a conventional fax machine, and are then optically scanned directly into Gulliver, converted into electronic transactions and processed. In the other direction, Gulliver replies by faxing suppliers to inform them of reservations, amendments or cancellations. In this way, smaller operations can have easy access to Gulliver with a minimum of technology.

### Tourism Brand Ireland

By all accounts, the re-engineered system was seen as a success. During 1995, IR£9 million worth of business was channelled through the system. It also formed a key element of initiatives such as the Bord Failte/NITB joint marketing campaign known as *Tourism Brand Ireland*. This focused on increasing customer satisfaction and loyalty, as well as attempting to build brand equity for the country as a whole and change its image into that of a young, dynamic and modern destination. One of its primary goals was to increase yield by attracting the higher-spending independent traveller. Initial reaction to the campaign has been very favourable. For example, Mr Patrick Coyle, chief executive of the Ryan Hotel Group has been quoted as saying: 'There is no doubt that Tourism Brand Ireland is working, even though it is massively under-funded. There is now a need to put the necessary funds behind it, and if that is done, it will pay big dividends for the tourism industry as a whole'.

At the same time, Gulliver was facing some further strategic challenges. Further investment was needed to continue its development and allow it to widen its channels of distribution. At the same time, the tourist boards were being downsized considerably and outsourcing many of their non-core activities, and thus were unable to contribute further funding. Gulliver also needed to start accepting bookings from outside the TIC network in order to help achieve critical mass. However, this posed legal and ethical issues, as tourist boards do not normally have a commercial mandate and thus reservations processing would have put them in competition with the private sector. For these reasons, the decision was taken to seek a strategic partner 'with proven capabilities in technology innovation and development to bring further investment and new skills to the Gulliver Team'.

Following a lengthy Europe-wide tendering process, a majority interest in Gulliver was acquired by FEXCO, a Kerry-based financial services, foreign exchange and call centre operation company. FEXCO was already heavily engaged in the tourism sector, with more than 2000 foreign exchange bureaux throughout Ireland and the UK. It also operates a centralized system to enable tourists to claim back the VAT – in a currency of their choice – on purchases made in Ireland, holds the Western Union franchise and provides international payment facilities for many Irish businesses. As such, it is an innovative company for whom the operation and development of Gulliver would offer great synergies. FEXCO is thought to have paid approximately IR£4 million for 74% of the new company while the tourist boards retained the remainder, thus ensuring that the interests of the industry are represented. Gulliver has thus been moved into the private sector, and its ongoing funding will come from membership fees, transaction fees, commissions and advertising revenue. As a result, the effectiveness and breadth of its channels of distribution are particularly important for its continued success.

### Expanding Routes to the Customer

While the initial Gulliver system was very successful in terms of providing an effective information system for use by TIC staff and thus improving visitor servicing, it only had a limited effect on making it easier to choose Ireland – the second of its key objectives. Only by continuing to develop its channels of distribution to include as broad an audience as possible can this be achieved. With this in mind, a variety of different distribution channels are being used today. These include:

- *TICs*: staff in TICs and RTOs located throughout the country can use the system to service visitor requests and make bookings at the more than 11,000 accommodation and 10,000 other tourism suppliers included on the system.
- *Market offices*: the overseas market offices of both Bord Failte and the NITB use the system to provide an information service to both consumers and the travel trade on all aspects of Irish tourism.
- *Tour operators*: leading tour operators in the UK and in France can use the system to book accommodation and other tourism services. This service will shortly be extended to other tour operators bringing travellers into Ireland.
- *Web site*: launched in 1996, the award-winning Tourism Brand Ireland Web site (www.ireland.travel.ie) allows potential customers anywhere in the world to find information about visiting Ireland. The site includes sections on places to stay and things to do, as well as information on how to get to Ireland and an innovative 'personal brochure and itinerary' feature. Visitors can either use the hyperlinks to browse through the site and find the information they require, or can use a powerful search engine to find more specific data. On-line availability and booking facilities will shortly be added, which will allow potential visitors to reserve accommodation and other services directly over the Web.
- *Telesales centre*: Gulliver forms a key component of the re-branding/promotional campaign known as *Tourism Brand Ireland*. Promotional material for this campaign in Ireland, the UK, the USA, France, Germany, Norway and Sweden features a localized toll-free number, which automatically routes the caller to an Irish-based call centre (see, for example, Fig. 3.C). This operates 24 hours per day, 7 days a week to handle enquiries and process bookings and is staffed by multilingual personnel.

The range and scope of distribution channels will continue to be developed in the future. For example, it is planned to further develop its Internet presence by constructing additional Web sites focused on different aspects of Irish tourism, thus helping to service niche mar-

**Fig. 3.C.** Ireland: awaken to a different world.

kets. Similarly, negotiations are in progress with third-party companies to develop and operate public multimedia kiosks which would be located at airports, ferry ports and railway stations. An Extranet is in development to facilitate tour operator access to the system, and a proposed link with the GDSs is also being examined, which would make the suppliers listed on Gulliver available to travel agents world-wide. In both the existing and the planned channels, the Gulliver system is used as the core technology – the engine, to use an analogy – to service visitor enquiries and to process reservations and is thus central to the distribution of Irish tourism.

In short, everyone benefits from using the Gulliver system. The tourism supplier gains a new, powerful, efficient and cost-effective channel of distribution that addresses a large audience of potential customers. Individual travellers can find the information they need quickly and easily, and can make bookings directly with suppliers. Tourism intermediaries such as travel agents and tour operators have simpler access to relevant, up-to-date information, and can check availability and make bookings at a relatively low cost. Lastly, the tourist boards benefit though a more cost-efficient and effective TIC network, and through effective distribution of Ireland's tourism products to both the internal and the external markets.

# Chapter 4

# Cutting out the Middleman! Tourism and the Internet

## 4.1 Introduction

One of the major limitations of all of the distribution channels discussed so far is that they, for the most part, all ultimately flow through the GDSs. As we have seen, this has several implications in terms of cost (as the GDS providers demand a fee for each transaction processed), audience (as GDSs are mostly used by travel agents and other business travel-orientated clients) and information content (GDS distribution is limited both in the data that can be distributed and by its textually based interface). As a result, many tourism suppliers would like to bypass the GDS route and use electronic distribution to sell directly to the consumer.

Until comparatively recently, no suitable technology had gained wide enough acceptance to allow this to happen. However, with the phenomenal growth in the use of the Internet and the World Wide Web both in the home and in the workplace, and the opportunities presented by falling hardware/communications costs, the potential now exists for tourism suppliers to both distribute information to and process reservations from customers directly. An entirely new form of travel distribution, dubbed 'alternative distribution systems' (ADS) by HEDNA, has developed and many of these use the Internet as their distribution medium (HEDNA, 1998b). This chapter examines the origins and development of Internet-based commerce, and assesses its implications (and potential future impact) on the tourism sector.

## 4.2 The Internet and the World Wide Web

The Internet has existed for some time, but has only come into the mainstream of business thinking comparatively recently. Put simply, it is a vast network of computer networks, linking computers in every corner of the globe so that they can communicate and share data with each other. Its structure (or rather lack of structure!) can best be described as being like 'a spaghetti bowl' – knowing no shape or bounds and having no centre, with networks being joined in an almost random fashion. It is not owned, managed or regulated by anybody, although various organizations voluntarily contribute services and systems which help to support its overall architecture (Cahill, 1995).

The origins of the Internet lie in a communications system known as ARPANET which was developed by the US military in the late 1960s. Mainframe computers were linked together to facilitate the sharing of data, but the links were deliberately designed to be fail safe and to have redundancy, so that if one part of the network was destroyed, messages could find an alternative route to their destination. Over time, its use spread from the military to other government departments, to non-government organizations such as universities and research laboratories, and ultimately to the business community and the general public.

Technically, communication over the Internet is facilitated by the use of a protocol known as *transmission control protocol/Internet protocol* or TCP/IP. All computers connected to the Internet use this to communicate with each other and to transport data. The major advantage of TCP/IP is that it is truly platform independent, which enables computers and networks of different shapes, sizes and structures to exchange data with one another. Thus, it doesn't matter if you are using an IBM PC or a Macintosh, are connected to a mainframe or are using a set-top browser box linked to your television set, the common protocol TCP/IP allows you to access and use the facilities of the Internet transparently. In effect, the Internet looks and behaves exactly the same on each of these devices, giving a vast potential audience for its content.

The Internet supports a wide variety of different tools and functions that can be used for communication or sharing data. These include electronic mail, Usenet, Gopher, Telnet and file transfer protocol (FTP). However, the use of many of these tools is relatively technical, a fact which kept the Internet within the domain of scientists and academics for decades. It was only the comparatively recent introduction of user-friendly graphical interfaces (in particular the 'World Wide Web') that captured the imagination of the public and opened up the Internet to mainstream use. The Web is, in essence, an overlay on top of the traditional Internet which is accessed using a piece of software known as a 'browser'. This reads, interprets and displays 'Web pages' which can contain full-colour graphics, sound and video in addition to the textual content traditionally associated with the Internet. Pages are written in *hypertext mark-up language* (HTML).

This started as an simple set of 'tags' that informed the browser software where to put italics, bold face, paragraph breaks, lines, graphics and other design elements in its display, but has since developed further to allow sound, moving graphics and various levels of interactivity to be incorporated into Web pages (Bathory-Kitsz, 1996). These pages of information do not have to be read sequentially. Instead, certain words (or graphics) can be designated as 'hyper-links'. When clicked-on, these transport the user to other pages, potentially stored in different places and on different computers. This non-linear arrangement allows users to skip from page to page and in effect 'navigate' their own path through the Web to find the information they require.

The exact size of the Internet is hard to quantify, partly because of its unstructured nature. However, the development and acceptance of the Web as the standard way of using the Internet has led to phenomenal interest on the part of the general public. Over the past 10 years, the Internet has grown from a size that could be measured in hundreds to one that must be measured in millions. Each network connected to the Internet could be composed of anywhere between a few and several thousand computers. Each of these could have several (or even several hundred) users, and thus establishing the total number of people using the Internet is practically an impossible task. Current estimates put it at over 50 million users, with growth rates of up to 15% per month (Breakwell, 1997). The futurist John Naisbitt argues that if the current rate of growth continues unabated, there will be over 300 million Internet users by 1999, 750 million by 2000 and 1.5 billion by 2001 (Naisbitt, 1994). Similarly, IBM has estimated that 10% of the world's population will have Internet access by the year 2000: that is, over 700 million people (Cahill, 1996). Irrespective of whose forecast is correct, what is clear is that the Internet will continue to increase in importance as a communications medium, and its potential for electronic commerce will continue to grow.

Instead of trying to estimate total numbers, many studies now focus on establishing the demographics of the Internet; establishing the gender, education, income, race, occupation and geographic traits of users. Some of the general conclusions from these studies indicate that males as opposed to females, people in higher as opposed to lower socio-economic groups and Caucasians as opposed to other racial groups are more likely to be Internet users. However, these demographics are shifting over time, with the demographic profile gradually becoming more mainstream (Schonland and Williams, 1996). However, even as the demographics currently stand, the typical profile of Web users matches that of the most desirable travel markets – affluent, highly educated, frequent travellers who spend above-average amounts on recreation and entertainment – in short, an ideal market for travel-related products (Dombey, 1998a). While 'hard goods' are thought to sell poorly online, services such as travel, where the product is less tangible and customers rely more on information, are more suited to the online environment. Recent research has shown that travel products are one of the most popular products purchased over the Web. Jupiter Communications estimate that over 800 million bookings were made over the Internet in 1997. Although this currently represents less than 1% of all travel revenues, by the year 2002 between 6% and 10% of travel reservations, representing sales of over $8 billion (Fig. 4.1), will originate on the Web (Travel Industry Association of America, 1998a).

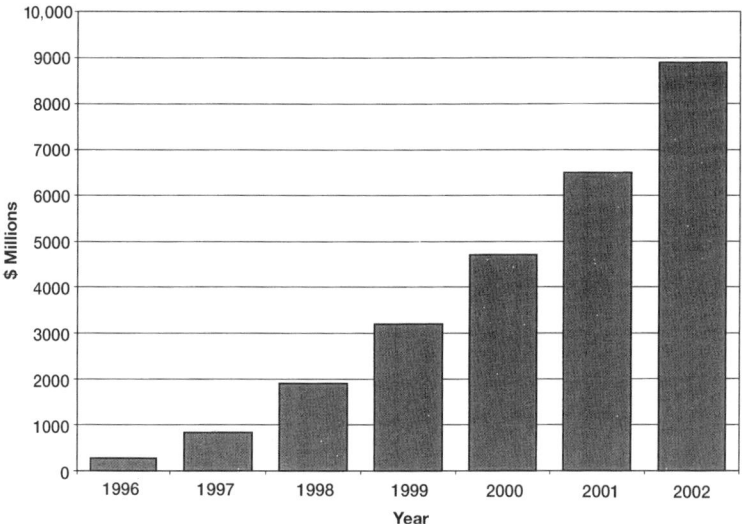

**Fig. 4.1.** Current and forecasted Internet travel revenues. Source: Jupiter Communications (1997).

## 4.3 Getting on to the Web

From the user's point of view, getting connected to the Web is easy. In many cases, their company's network may already be connected to the Internet, and thus the user can get access from their workplace simply by installing suitable software (such as a Web browser and an Email client). From home, the user also needs a modem and an account with an *internet service provider* (ISP) – a company that offers access to the Internet over a dial-up telephone connection. For the supplier, however, access is more complicated as there is a wide variety of choices available, depending on the level of service and facilities they wish to offer.

The conventional approach is for companies to set up their own

Web server. To do this, they require the use of a relatively powerful computer, special Web server software and a dedicated leased telephone line to permanently connect the server to the Internet. Obviously, a certain amount of technical knowledge is also required to get (and keep!) the system up and running. As such, this approach is relatively expensive, but does have the benefits of having a 'marketable' Web address (for example, www.abc-hotels.com) and being able to use the full range of facilities and features of Web technologies to help enhance your Web site and engage in electronic commerce (Ginsburg, 1997). The alternative is to rent space from a ISP and, in effect, share a Web server with other companies. While this is considerably cheaper, in effect it limits Web efforts to just displaying static Web pages as the facilities needed to develop interactive features are generally not available with this solution. In addition, the resulting Web address is usually much less attractive from a promotional point of view. Instead of www.abc-hotels.com, a company could end up with something like members.aol.com~abc-hotels or abc-hotels.demon.co.uk, which does not do much for its corporate image. A recent development that represents a compromise between these two extremes may be a useful alternative. Many ISPs have introduced 'virtual servers'; a technology which allows several companies to share the same physical server but, at the same time, appear to the outside world as if they have their own facilities. Companies can register their own Web address, and can also have access to the full range of server facilities, and all at a fraction of the cost of purchasing and maintaining their own equipment.

Irrespective of the method of getting access to the Web, the next step is the creation of the company's Web pages. As has been discussed, pages are written in HTML, which can either be written manually, or can be generated by a variety of easy-to-use Web editing software packages. However, this approach requires a significant amount of ongoing support and maintenance. Considerable time must be spent updating and managing increasing quantities of obsolete information, rather than on adding new content (and therefore value) to the site. To put this message crudely, if a site has just three pages that are not likely to change, a user is unlikely to visit it repeatedly – one visit and they will feel that they know its entire scope (Dorren and Slater, 1996). This maintenance problem is considerable when you consider that all but the simplest sites contain hundreds or thousands of HTML pages, and thus updating this volume of information using conventional manual editing techniques is impossible (IMRG, 1996). In addition, a lot of tourism-related data is particularly dynamic. Information on, for example, availability or rates are constantly changing, and thus need to be updated regularly. In many cases, these data are already stored electronically on another computerized system (such as a PMS or a CRS). Advanced Web technologies such as *CGI scripting* can be used to give Web users access to this information automatically, without the need to create a Web page manually. Requests from the user's Web browser are translated into a query, which is passed on to the underlying database. The answer generated is then automatically converted to HTML 'on-the-fly', and dispatched back to the user where it appears as a page in their Web browser. Although there are some speed penalties, the resulting pages are dynamic and always contain up-to-date information, and the entire process happens automatically without having to manually update Web pages (Bathory-Kitsz, 1996).

## 4.4 Internet Difficulties

The Internet is not, however, without its problems. Foremost among these is the difficulty which users have in finding relevant information. The Web offers a vast, rich universe of information; 320 million pages is a recently quoted figure (KPMG, 1998). However, there is no single entry point or centralized directory of content. Each site is free to develop its own hierarchy of information. This unstructured nature makes it difficult and confusing for novice and experienced users alike to locate the information they want. Although the development of search engines and content-based directories (such as Altavista and Yahoo, respectively) has made finding information somewhat simpler, it is still easy to get distracted or lost during a search. Therefore actually getting the customer to visit your site can be troublesome. As can be seen from Fig. 4.2, unless they know your Web address in advance, their search will invariably involve multiple search steps, during which they could easily defect to competitors or become distracted by totally different topics. Ironically, the most effective way to build awareness of sites seems to be through publicizing them through traditional media channels such as in print advertisements, in brochures and on business cards (Hyung-Soo and Baker, 1998).

Another limiting factor is speed. The performance of the Web has become so poor that in many circles it has been christened the 'World Wide Wait'! Its speed problems have two underlying causes. The first stems from the constantly growing number of Internet users. Because more and more people are sharing the same resources, the communication channels are becoming increasingly crowded, and thus simply cannot cope with the increased traffic. Congestion means that it takes longer for information to travel over the Internet, as there is usually a queue for communication resources. The second part of the problem is caused by the fact that the information being transported has become 'richer'. In the early days of the Internet, only textual data were

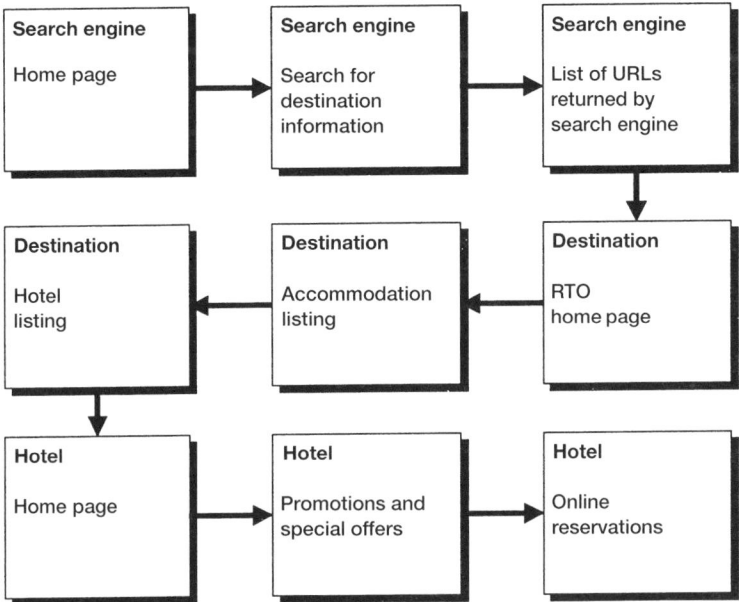

**Fig. 4.2.** A hypothetical search illustrating the steps from the initial search for information to making a reservation. Source: adapted from Bender (1997a).

being sent from computer to computer. Now, encouraged by marketing professionals more used to designing glossy magazine adverts, full-colour pictures, animation, sound and even video are routinely being transported over the same routes, adding to the congestion problem. Even while using high-speed modems and fast connections, users often experience significant delays when accessing Web sites. This has important psychological implications as customers often differentiate between tourism suppliers based on speed of service. Consequently, slow response times could reflect poorly on an operation's image. Using text-only displays is not the answer, as the Web loses much of its appeal without its graphical and other 'rich media' enhancements. The challenge for the Web marketer is to find an appropriate balance between text and graphics so that the user is attracted to the site but can still access the information in a reasonable time frame (Cho *et al.*, 1995).

The last major problem is probably the most pressing. Correctly or incorrectly, there is a perception among the general public that the Web is insecure. Although many people would like to purchase travel services directly, and are actively searching for relevant products, at present they do not seem willing to complete the transaction by sending their credit card details over the Internet. This perception has delayed the widespread diffusion of electronic commerce not only in the travel sector but in business in general. However, the security systems and technology needed to permit safe credit card transactions over the Internet are rapidly being developed (Walle, 1996). The association of trusted brands such as the SET (Secure Electronic Transactions) standard, developed jointly by Visa and MasterCard is helping to reduce consumer's security fears (KPMG, 1998). More effective 'firewalls', increased use of encryption and increased technology literacy will also help to increase consumer confidence. Perhaps the situation is best summed up by John Cahill, Senior Vice President of Management Information Systems for Inter-Continental Hotels, and an outspoken critic of tourism distribution on the Internet in the past:

> The power of the Internet is growing. Its problems are diminishing and its potential is vast. How you deal with this latest hospitality technology and sales phenomenon may mean the difference between not meeting your goals or exceeding them as we rapidly approach the new millennium.
>
> (Cahill, 1996).

## 4.5 Marketing on the Web

Much of the 'hype' surrounding the Web focuses on its potential for both electronic marketing and electronic commerce. Certainly, most people would agree that the Web constitutes an important new channel of distribution, which provides marketers with a powerful and direct channel with which to interact with consumers (Murphy *et al.*, 1996a). However, the Web is unlike any other channel that has existed in the past. It has several characteristics that make traditional marketing practices ineffective, and sometimes even counter productive. The hospitality marketer needs to take these unique features into account in order to gain maximum benefit from this powerful new electronic medium.

One of the most important characteristics of the Web is its global market reach. Putting your company's information on the Web gives it unparalleled exposure, as it is instantly available to potential customers worldwide, 24 hours a day, 365 days a year. Customers anywhere can access your promotional material at a time that is convenient for them, and thus do not have to struggle to contact sales people during office hours (Bender, 1997a). Promotional literature can make use of the full capabilities of the Web by incorporating full-colour photographs and graphics, sound, animation and even video, all at a fraction of the cost of producing paper-based brochures. These multimedia brochures can be updated quickly, easily and as often as necessary, which gives great potential for promoting last-minute offers.

For example, British Airways have traditionally used newspaper and television advertising to promote last-minute sales. However, the immediacy of the Web offers them more flexibility, and is now used as their preferred way of getting special offers out into the marketplace (Huddart, 1998).

The traditional way to market to a large audience is to use a 'broadcasting' approach; essentially to use a single, standardized ('one size fits all') message which is designed to appeal to your broad target market. The marketer controls the content (the information which is presented), the timing (when it is seen), the location (where it is seen) as well as the frequency (how often it is seen). Print and television advertising are common examples of this type of promotion. Content is limited by factors such as the cost and capacity, and in any case, the strategy often results in a great deal of wasted exposure (Meijer, 1995). In most cases, the marketer has little idea who will see their glossy (and expensive) advertisements, and it is a waste of resources to pitch advertising at people outside the target audience. Even when it is targeted correctly, advertising of this type is often ineffective because it fails to engage the customer. As they have no personal involvement, the advertisement does not entice them to purchase the product.

Web marketing, however, turns many of these characteristics upside down. Firstly, with a Web presentation, it is the customer, not the marketer, who is in control. Using hyper-links, customers determine what they will view, when they will view it (if at all) and even the direction and order in which the information is presented (Bender, 1995). If they do not like what they find, they can be gone in a single click, so the notion of a passive captive audience does not apply on the Web (Hoffman and Novak, 1996). An electronic version of a conventional printed brochure and promotional materials is not enough; content and format need to be adapted to take advantage of the power of the Web, and navigation tools need to be included to prevent users getting lost in the data. A Web site's content should be relevant to the viewers' needs, easy to use and should include logical links to areas of further interest. Simply getting the user to visit a site once is also ineffective. Its content must change regularly, and must be absorbing enough to make users want to come back again and again (Deighton, 1996).

Secondly, unlike traditional direct marketing techniques, it is the customer who comes to the company for information, not vice versa. The marketer is not blindly sending out mailings, hoping that they will reach someone who is interested in their subject. On the Web, it is the customer who is actively searching for information (Werthner, 1997). In effect, they are 'pre-screened', because, by visiting the Web site, they are showing both interest and involvement – they have a need for information (and hopefully your product) and are likely to buy from whoever best satisfies this need. The fact that they have chosen to visit and are not being compelled to do so (as may be the case with television advertisements) is significant. The Web, therefore, gives a company access to persons who are already predisposed to learning more about its products – a very desirable situation. Even when traditional advertising principles are being used on the Web, such as with banner advertising or push technology, it is precisely targeted at people who have previously demonstrated an interest in the product. For example, with search engines such as Yahoo and Altavista, a user who runs a query for sites relating to travel in Ireland can be presented with a banner advert for an Irish hotel chain along with the search results. The advertising message is not being randomly 'pushed' at the customer – they are actively seeking to pull it in (Bender, 1997a).

Thirdly, Web promotion does not suffer from the size or capacity constraints imposed by printing costs or advertising space. The cost of building additional pages is very low, and thus, in the electronic world, it is possible to include very comprehensive information cheaply. Furthermore, unlike most other forms of marketing and promotion, expenditure on Web marketing is not used up in a single instance. With, for example, newspaper advertising, your marketing efforts are sitting in a rubbish bin the next day. A Web page, on the other hand, continues working for you until you decide to remove it or you change it. By hyper-linking pages together in an appropriate fashion, the Web marketer can create an ultra-comprehensive personalized multimedia brochure that is instantly available to potential customers worldwide (Bender, 1997b). This allows viewers to take a tailor-made tour and explore your products and services based on their individual needs and interests, not based on a standardized mass market sales message. Widely different information requirements can be easily and economically accommodated. Instead of having a single message targeting many customers, many different messages can be aimed at individual customers for a very low marginal cost. Such a personalized 'sniper' approach allows customers to get the information they want quickly and easily and is acknowledged to be more effective than traditional 'shotgun' methods, but could never be achieved using conventional marketing methods.

Other characteristics of the Web further facilitate this personalized approach. In addition to its potential for 'narrow-casting', the ability of the Web to facilitate two-way communication is a useful marketing tool. This two-way dialogue forms an important component of relationship marketing, and is an important factor in building customer loyalty. Customers can effortlessly communicate with companies to find product information, ask questions or negotiate prices, all with just a few keystrokes. Just as easily, companies can contact customers

**Table 4.1.** Six levels of Web interactivity. Source: adapted from Bathory-Kitsz (1996).

| Level | Description | Features |
|---|---|---|
| 1 | Static Web pages | Text, pictures, frames |
| 2 | Quasi-static Web pages | Maps, forms, animation, CGI |
| 3 | Active Web pages | Java applets, Server Push, recorded audio and video |
| 4 | Quasi-interactive Web pages | User detection, on-the-fly page creation |
| 5 | Interactive Web pages | Interactive audio and video, remote applications |
| 6 | The future? | Voice recognition, virtual reality |

to clarify their needs or inform them of new products. Features such as Email, Web forms, CGI and Java applets positively encourage marketers to interact with consumers. As Deighton (1996) points out, interactivity of this type is high-tech, and can be 'as subtle, as flexible, as pertinent and as persuasive as in a one on one dialogue' (Table 4.1). The computer can also remember the individual's responses, which in turn makes it possible to customize the messages flowing back to the customer to reflect their individual likes and preferences. This high level of responsiveness makes the Web unique among marketing media. Perhaps Microsoft Expedia, the travel service of the Microsoft Network (www.expedia.com), provides the ultimate travel-related example of this phenomenon. This Web site tracks the actions of users and assesses their preferences and travel habits based on the pages they access and the products they book. Expedia then maintains contact with each user by sending periodic Email messages, which are automatically customized to match that individual's interests and buying habits, thus helping to reinforce the relationship and making the user return to the Web site.

One of the benefits of Web marketing is that the effectiveness of promotion can be determined relatively quickly and precisely (Pollock, 1997c). Web servers can provide valuable usage statistics and show which pages are being accessed by customers. With Web-based promotion, you can tell who is looking at your information, where they came from, what pages they look at and the order in which they access them. Unlike with a printed brochure, you can tell that no one reads the page about the restaurant or that people go to the information about your facilities first, and then look at the information about location. A good example of how this information can be used is provided by the Best Western hotel chain, which began their Internet presence by loading 160 of its properties on to the Travelweb site (www.travelweb.com). Within the first month, they had more than

80,000 hits or accesses, and the system provided an electronic address for each individual who accessed their data. From this, Best Western could figure out that about half of its viewers were from outside the US and the bulk were individual, not institutional or corporate users – characteristics of their market that would have been difficult to establish using conventional channels (Rowe, 1995). They were also able to tell that few users looked at information about and pictures of bedrooms in their hotels, indicating that such information was not as important as previously thought in the promotion of their product.

Marketing over the Internet is not, of course, limited solely to information distribution – it also has acknowledged direct-selling potential. It removes the geographical boundaries and physical barriers that traditionally separate the buyer and seller, thus changing the way in which many products are distributed. For example, in a hotel scenario, the visitor might use the Web to find and browse properties which matched his interest, compare facilities and prices and then might decide to make a reservation, guaranteeing it with a credit card (Roache, 1997). However, even though the technology to permit such transactions exists, the general public has, to date, largely failed to embrace it. Suppliers, too, have been slow to take advantage of the opportunities presented by electronic commerce. For example, a 1996 survey of hotel sites found that while over half claimed to offer the means to make a reservation, only half of these had a functioning reservations system, less than one-quarter suggested how to make payment for the reservation and less than 5% offered a secure method for making payment directly via the Web site (Murphy *et al.*, 1996b). Similarly, a 1997 UK-focused survey found that only 21% of hotel chains offered real-time processing of reservations (Gilbert *et al.*, 1998). Clearly there is a difference between accepting reservations and completing the transaction, and most hotel sites do not appear to have yet made the distinction. The lack of such facilities means that the customer has to wait for confirmation. Since one of the primary attractions of the Web is its interactivity, many could be disappointed.

Although direct selling is developing more slowly than the information distribution function of the Web, the potential for electronic commerce is vast. The advantages for tourism suppliers are great; the automated process means little, if any, labour costs. Also, because the Web is a direct channel, travel agent commission is eliminated. All in all, an Internet booking is estimated to cost about 20% of one processed through a CRO (Cahill, 1996); and the volume of bookings can only rise as new methods of accessing the Web, such as Web-enabled televisions, cellular phones, personal digital assistants (PDAs) and other devices gain widespread acceptance. As a result, practically all the actors in the tourism industry are scrambling to establish an Internet presence. While few see it as becoming a mainstream channel in the near future, no one wants to risk being left behind (Arthur Andersen, 1998).

## 4.6 Tourism on the World Wide Web

One of the problems in attempting to assess the impact of the Internet and the World Wide Web on the tourism sector is its phenomenal growth rate. Statistics change daily, and thus are inaccurate even before they are published. However, one trend is clear – all the major players in the tourism sector are getting online. In January 1996, the consultants Arthur Andersen estimated that there were about 5000 travel-related sites: by 1998 this figure had risen to more than 80,000 (Arthur Andersen, 1998). Table 4.2 illustrates the sheer scope of travel distribution on the Web. Based on an extract from the Yahoo directory, although it is not all-inclusive, it gives some idea of the range and diversity of travel services that can be found online.

Instead of talking in terms of numbers, perhaps a more interesting analysis is to examine and classify tourism Web sites into generic categories based on the type of companies who operate them. Basically, sites can be categorized into those operated by travel suppliers or those operated by intermediaries. The former can again be subdivided into those operated by the major international multi-unit chains and those operated by independent companies.

The first category – chain sites – includes those of the major hotel companies and the car rental companies. These typically promote and distribute information about a single type of product (e.g. hotel rooms or rental cars) and only the products of a single company. The budget tourism sector (such as for example, airlines like Southwest Airways or hotel chains such as Formule 1), whose margins are too small to allow them to afford to distribute over traditional electronic channels, are particularly interested in the potential of the Internet for distribution (Fig. 4.3).

**Table 4.2.** Number of travel sites on the Web. Source: based on an extract from the Yahoo Web director (www.yahoo.com), July 1998.

| Type | Number | Type | Number |
|---|---|---|---|
| Airlines | 492 | Hostels | 107 |
| Bed and breakfasts | 1759 | Resorts | 219 |
| Bus companies | 13 | Reservation services | 24 |
| Casinos | 70 | Timeshare companies | 64 |
| Car rental firms | 36 | Tour operators | 2374 |
| Cruise companies | 345 | Travel agents | 1315 |
| Hotels | 426 | Trains and railways | 58 |

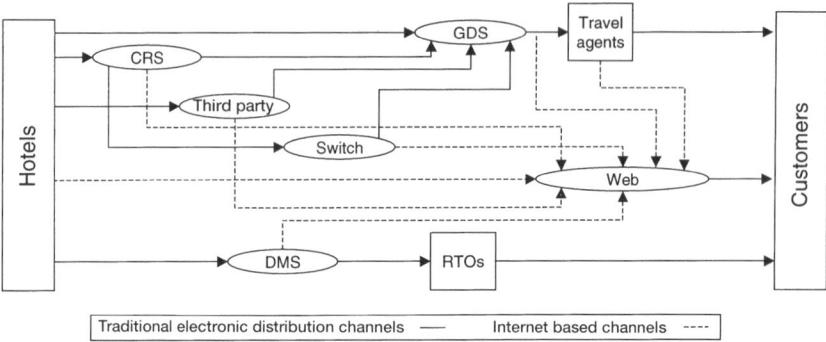

**Fig. 4.3.** Traditional electronic vs. Internet-based distribution channels.

Most chains provide a central site containing information on the company in general, and on corporate-wide schemes, such as loyalty clubs, special promotions, corporate partnerships, etc. (Tellini, 1995). Most include a search engine, which makes it easy for potential customers to find the product that meets their needs. To use a hotel example, users enter the location and any other desired criteria (such as having a swimming pool or baby-sitting facilities) into a Web page-based form, and the site responds with a list of the properties which meet their needs. Profiles of each property can usually be displayed, which typically include textual descriptions supplemented by photos and, on more advanced systems, availability/rate data and online reservation facilities. These can range in complexity from printed forms that the user can print out and fax back to the company for processing, to an Email hyperlink that allows the user to request further information or an online form that accesses an interactive inventory database and is capable of processing the entire booking (Table 4.3). Certain companies are also using their Web sites as a channel for disposing of distressed inventory, either by advertising last-minute availability special offers or through 'cyberauctions' (Arthur Andersen, 1998). For example, American Airlines runs its highly successful 'NetSaver' promotion each Wednesday to dispose of unsold seats for the following weekend. The scheme has resulted in the carrier selling all seats on some flights, boosting load factors from around 65% to nearly 100% (Jennings, 1996).

Sites for independent tourism suppliers tend to be more varied and harder to find. Most sites tend to contain only a few static Web pages, but sometimes the flexibility of not having to conform to corporate guidelines means that smaller operations can have innovative, effective and comprehensive sites. A good example of such a case is

**Table 4.3.** Reservation services on leading hotel chain Web sites. Ranking based on *Hotels*, July 1997, p. 48.

| Rank | Hotel chain | Web site URL | Reservation method |
|---|---|---|---|
| 1 | Cendant Corp. / HFS Inc. | Brand-based, e.g. www.ramamda.com | Online reservations through TravelWeb |
| 2 | Holiday Inn Worldwide | www.holiday-inn.com | Online reservations |
| 3 | Best Western International | www.bestwestern.com | CRO telephone number |
| 4 | Groupe Accor | www.hotelweb.fr | Via Email or CRO telephone number |
| 5 | Choice Hotels | www.hotelchoice.com | Online reservations |
| 6 | Marriott International | www.marriott.com | Online reservations through TravelWeb |
| 7 | ITT Sheraton Corp. | www.ITTSheraton.com | Online reservations |
| 8 | Promus Cos. | Brand-based, e.g. www.embassy-suites.com | Online reservations through TravelWeb |
| 9 | Hilton Hotels Corp. | www.hilton.com | Online reservations |
| 10 | Carlson Hospitality | Brand-based, e.g. www.raddison.com | Online reservations |
| 11 | Hyatt Hotels | www.hyatt.com | Online reservations through TravelWeb |
| 12 | Inter-Continental Hotels | www.interconti.com | Online reservations through TravelWeb |
| 13 | Hilton International | www.hilton.com | Online reservations |
| 14 | Grupo Sol Melia | www.solmelia.es | Online reservations |
| 15 | Forte Hotels | www.forte-hotels.com | Online reservations through Travelocity |

provided by Tellini in his discussion of the site for The Vicarage Hotel in London (http://londonvicarage.com):

> The site is separated into various sections. The first is the *Introduction* which gives information on The Vicarage itself. Room rates and breakfast menu are presented in the *Details* section. *Highlights* include information on Notting Hill Carnival and New Year's Eve in Trafalgar Square. *Directions* are given from the airport and the Tube. *Frequently Asked Questions* presents a list, with questions ranging from check-in times to the parking situation. A guide for *What's On In London* with information on the Tube and London Museums is included, as well as pictures of Vicarage employees, the view from the B&B and The Vicarage's taxi man.

Perhaps the success of this Web site is best measured by the number of bookings it creates. After 2 months of operation, bookings originating on the Web outstripped its previous number one source of bookings at The Vicarage. Some of the reasons for its success may be that it includes information not only on the B&B itself, but also general tourist information on the surrounding area. It also does this in a very user-friendly manner, which encourages use by people new to the Web.

### 4.6.1 Travel Mega Sites

At the outset of the Internet travel phenomenon, most observers predicted that the major travel agency chains would become the leaders in the provision of online travel sales. However, with the exception of American Express, it seems that most have failed to exploit this opportunity successfully. Instead, new companies are emerging and dominating the marketplace. As can be seen from Table 4.4, the majority of these are comprehensive sites, offering a broad range of services and products and with the potential to replace the traditional travel agent.

The basic concept behind these Mega sites is that of an integrated virtual travel mall – combining travel products from different sources and offering the user a standard mechanism to search through information and order products (Bloch *et al.*, 1996b). Despite the novelty of the concept and the relative immaturity of the sites, they are having a dramatic impact, with sites such as Travelocity, Microsoft Expedia and Preview Travel selling in the region of $1–2 million worth of tickets each per week (*The Economist*, 10–16 May 1998). Several of these sites have their origins in the GDSs, who are attempting to leverage their existing investments in reservation systems to reach the customer directly. Such sites offer a full travel service, and allow users to search for information on flights, car rental and hotels using the same databases available to travel agents over their terminals but with a more friendly user interface. With hotel or car hire bookings, the user can usually complete the entire process through the site and receive online confirmation. However, with flights, because of international regulations governing air transportation, the booking is usually transferred to the travel agency associated with the site for ticketing.

A common characteristic of successful Mega sites is the range of useful resources that they provide for the traveller in addition to their 'commercial' information. These often include general travel advice, destination guides containing information on area attractions, travel news, local weather reports, currency converters, location maps and even point-to-point driving instructions (Pusateri and Manno, 1998). Such features have been included to broaden the range of services provided for the potential customer, thus helping to make the site their

**Table 4.4.** Top ten most visited travel Web sites. Source: adapted from Wardell (1998).

| Rank | Name | URL | Description |
|---|---|---|---|
| 1 | Microsoft Expedia | www.expedia.com | Travel Mega site offering information and reservations for flights, hotels, car hire and packages through a variety of partner suppliers, including Worldspan for flights and TravelWeb for hotels |
| 2 | Travelocity | www.travelocity.com | Travel Mega site offering information and reservations for flights, hotels and car hire, based on the SABRE GDS |
| 3 | Excite City.Net | www.city.net | Information-focused site (based on its search engine origins), offering reservations facilities through Preview Travel (no. 10 on the list) |
| 4 | United Airlines | www.ual.com | Airline site offering information and online flight reservations |
| 5 | Map Quest | www.mapquest.com | Information-focused site offering maps and some travel planning services |
| 6 | Asia Travel | www.asiatravel.com | Geographically focused hotel and resort information |
| 7 | American Airways | www.americanair.com | Airline site offering information about the company's products and services, and a more extensive range of benefits (including reservation facilities) to AAdvantage Club members |
| 8 | Carnival Cruise Lines | www.carnival.com | A promotional site for the world's largest cruise company |
| 9 | Intellicast | www.intellicast.com | Information-focused site, mainly containing destination information and weather |
| 10 | Preview Travel | www.previewtravel.com | Travel Mega site, with the ability to book flights, hotels, car hire and packages |

central source of travel information and relieving them of the need to consult any other intermediary.

Travel distribution on the Internet is still in its infancy, and while no one is sure what will eventually be the most effective strategy to adopt, it is clear that the Web is causing many of the traditional distribution channels to become less well defined. These developments have resulted in considerable debate as to the future of the traditional intermediaries. Why should a customer use the services of a travel agent or tour operator when they can find and book travel services themselves? Do such companies have a future in the 'wired world'?

## 4.7 Disintermediation?

As we have seen, one of the key benefits of Web distribution is its direct route to the customer. Great cost savings can be achieved by encouraging the customer to book electronically, which has made many tourism suppliers very excited about this new distribution channel. However, most companies also recognize the continuing importance of both the tour operator and travel agent, particularly given that direct booking has yet to achieve its full potential. Some, for example, Novotel, have chosen to respond by not providing booking facilities on their Web sites for fear of offending their travel agent partners (Murphy *et al.*, 1996a, b). Others have focused specific portions of their site specifically on the needs of these intermediaries. For example, Almo Rent-A-Car gained significant benefits by introducing real-time availability and online booking facilities for tour operators on their Web site – a move which helped them to reduce their administration expenses by over $1 million. Meanwhile, their tour operator partners are also estimated to have experienced a similar reduction in costs because of their ability to find information and make bookings with Almo in this way (Bender, 1997a). Other intermediaries are actively promoting the Web as a distribution channel to travel agents. Pegasus not only allows travel agents to book hotels over its TravelWeb site and collect their regular commission by adding their agency identification number to the booking, but is actually paying an incentive to encourage agents to book in this way rather than through their GDS or by phone (Pegasus Systems, 1998).

The response of travel agents to the threat of disintermediation has been denial. They claim that agencies have two distinct roles: helping suppliers to market their products and services while simultaneously serving the needs of travellers (Walle, 1996). While the Web has an effect on the latter role, they feel that their greatest strength has always been their ability to collate, organize and interpret large amounts of data in a way that delivers the best value and the most exciting travel experiences for the customer. While the Web provides information, this is not the same as knowledge. A customer can download pages and pages of information about a destination from the Web, but this is no match for the first-hand experience of a knowledgeable agent when it comes to recommending the hotels, restaurants and amenities which best match that customer's needs. In addition, agents feel that customers have neither the time nor the incentive to browse the Web for travel information, and that the information overload

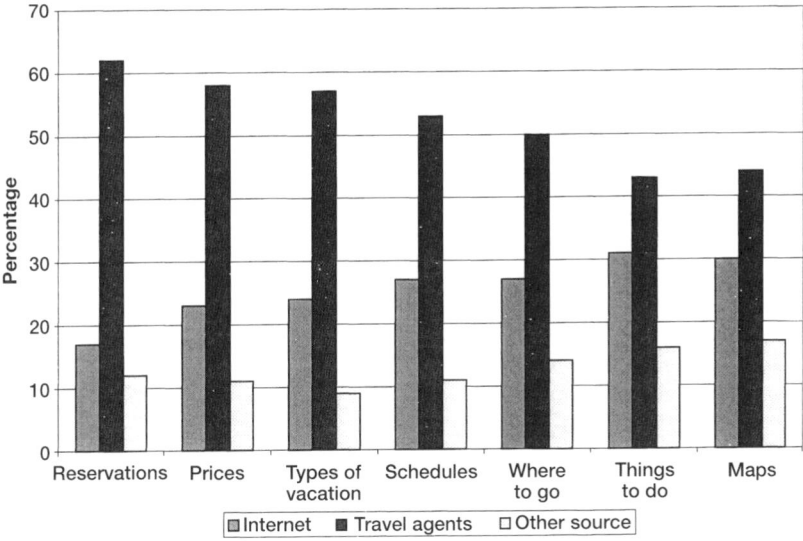

**Fig. 4.4.** Preferred source for travel information (1997). Source: Travel Industry Association of America (1998a).

which the Web is creating is 'driving customers into their waiting arms, rather than away' (Knodt, 1997). This view is supported by recent research carried out by the US-based Travel Industry Association (Fig. 4.4). This revealed that while the use of online travel services is growing, travellers in general prefer to rely on travel agents rather than online travel services for each of seven different types of transactions (Travel Industry Association of America, 1998b).

In addition, many agencies are themselves starting to use the Internet, either by setting up online agencies, or by using the Web as an additional information resource to help better service their clients. While many of these sites perform the traditional travel agency functions of acting as an information conduit between supplier and customers, making bookings and issuing tickets, increasingly their focus is more on adding value by acting as a navigator through the maze of travel information that is available (Bloch, 1996). As travel continues to become more global, and as destinations and travel suppliers make more and more travel products available online, it is indeed likely that consumers will need such data navigators to scan, locate and retrieve the information they need (Pollock, 1995a).

The counter argument is that travellers only patronise agencies to acquire information that helps to reduce the risk involved in travel. When the services which agencies offer are no longer regarded as being important, or when they are no longer perceived as being the most convenient way to get this information, customers will go elsewhere. As the power of the Internet grows, it will become easier to find information, and more convenient to book electronically.

Additional threats will present themselves as more and more non-tourism companies enter the marketplace. Unhampered by old habits and an expensive high street infrastructure of retail outlets, such companies bring different experiences, resources, client bases and competitive strategies to the industry, and also do not have historic relationships with any of the major players (Reinders and Baker, 1998). As a result, they can introduce substantial changes without worrying about 'treading on people's toes'. A prime example of such a company is Microsoft, which has entered the travel sector with its *Expedia* product and quickly captured a large market share. Intermediaries therefore have every right to be worried because, as their traditional roles are eliminated or absorbed by other members of the distribution chain, they will need to find another way of serving the customer if they are to remain in business.

## 4.8 Conclusion

As we have seen, the Internet has the potential to have a major effect on the way in which hospitality and tourism products are distributed by redefining how travellers discover and purchase tourism products. It has the potential to overcome many of the problems associated with the more traditional electronic distribution media (Mutch, 1996). By addressing itself directly to the consumer, it bypasses the GDS, thus giving rise to substantially lower costs and makes it possible to distribute low-margin products. The absence of requirements in terms of structure gives it the flexibility to distribute heterogeneous products, while the simplicity and general acceptance of its standardized user interface introduces consistency in how information is accessed – a necessary prerequisite for use by the travel trade. Its ease of entry, low set-up costs and the fact that no special equipment is needed make it attractive as a distribution medium for smaller tourism operations, while its multimedia capabilities and its global reach make it very effective as a marketing medium.

Its potential has been formally recognized by the tourism sector. At a major think tank sponsored by the International Hotel and Restaurant Association in 1997, it was forecast that the Internet would be the key driving force in the future tourism sector. In addition to giving rise to more demanding customers armed with instant access to information, it will also facilitate the creation of a marketplace where 'a segment of one' is the norm. Only those operations which can harness technology to correctly identify these customers' needs and customize their product accordingly will survive (WTO, 1997b).

# Case Study 8: Degriftour

## www.degriftour.fr

Degriftour, a French company based in Cergy Pontoise, north of Paris, have become one of the innovators in the use of electronic commerce in the tourism sector. Using new technology, they have begun to redefine the normal channels of distribution used for travel and entertainment products. From the very outset, their direction has been clear. They see themselves as being 'specialists in discounted travel sales, working with one simple concept – no shops, no retailers, no printed catalogues – just electronic communications and media'. As such, they represent the first and probably the most successful example of a 'virtual' travel agency. The success of both the company and the concept is shown by its results. In 1997, 145,000 customers booked through Degriftour and its associated brands Reductour and Club Bonjour France. Sales totalled over 330 million francs, representing over 5.5 million connections by Minitel as well as nearly half a million over the Web. The company also has very high brand recognition in France, with one in three people being familiar with the service (Fig. 4.A).

## Company Background

Established in 1991, Degriftour began by selling discounted tour packages to the French public. Its concept was to source last-minute availability for the different products that make up a package (flights, transfers and hotel accommodation), combine them together and offer them to the public at a discounted price. Suppliers benefited as Degriftour offered them an additional way to dispose of unreserved inventory that might not otherwise be sold, while the public benefited from lower prices if they were willing to wait and book at the last minute.

Degriftour quickly realized that only an electronic medium could be used to distribute their product successfully. The traditional printed catalogue normally used by tour operators would take too long to produce and would be too costly to be economical for use with their

This case study was prepared by Peter O'Connor, Assistant Professor, Institut de Management Hôtelier International (IMHI), as a basis for discussion rather than to illustrate either effective or ineffective handling of an administrative problem.

**Fig. 4.A.** Degriftour Web site home page.

discounted product. Similarly, distribution through travel agents or through their own retail outlets would also be too costly. What was needed was a low-cost, flexible distribution channel that could be used to target consumers directly and allow them to book quickly and easily. Fortunately, France had exactly such a distribution channel with its Minitel teletext network, which was being used for informational and commerce purposes on a daily basis by millions of French people. Making use of this network made Degriftour's products available to a wide audience 24 hours a day, 7 days per week. Bookings could be processed over the Minitel system, with the client entering their own address and credit card information, thus helping to keep data entry costs to a minimum. Travel documents such as the itinerary were send to the client by fax, and tickets were mailed or could be picked up at the airport, thus reducing physical interactions with the customer. As a result, the need for high street offices was eliminated as all transactions were processed electronically.

### Innovative Products

Degriftour are an extremely forward-thinking company, and have expanded the Degriftour concept to incorporate other related services. However, they have also remained true to their core concept – electronic distribution of discounted travel products. Some of Groupe Degriftour's current products include the following:

#### *Degriftour*

As discussed above, the Degriftour concept is one of discounted packages that are placed on the market 15 days before departure and can be booked until the day prior to departure. On average, 1200 different products are available, of which 300–400 change each day. Prices are usually 30–40% off rack rate, and payment in full must occur at time of booking. Variations of the basic service are also operated to service niche markets (e.g. DEGRIFNEIGE for winter sports, DEGRIFMER for river and sea cruises and DEGRIFTOUR LUXE for more upscale packages).

#### *Reductour*

The Reductour concept is also focused on package holidays but is aimed at people who do not want to wait until the last minute to book. As with a 'normal' tour operator, packages can be booked up to 6 months in advance, again at discounted prices (normally between 5% and 30% off the normal selling price). Reductour has on average 60,000 products in its database at any one time. Payment of 15% of the total purchase price must be made at the time of booking, with the balance due 1 month before departure.

### Sortez

Sortez was launched in 1995 and electronically distributes last-minute availability of all types of live shows, including theatre, cabaret, opera, ballet, modern dance, concerts, etc., mainly in the Paris area. The catalogue is updated three times daily, and allows customers to select performances up to 3 days in advance. Sortez gives customers a discount of 40% off the regular published price. Tickets are paid for by credit card at the time of booking, and Minitel generates a reservation number that the customer can then use to pick up the tickets at the theatre box office.

### Grandes Tables!

Grandes Tables! focuses on the restaurant sector, selling special offers at leading French restaurants at very competitive prices. The scheme was conceived in association with *Gault Millau* to allow restaurants to increase business during 'slow' periods. Each participating restaurant is among the best in France, with a grade of at least 17 out of 20 and three chefs' hats needed to participate in the scheme. On selected dates, these leading restaurants prepare a special 'degustation' menu (including pre-dinner drinks, wine and coffee) which is sold electronically for about 500 francs. As these menus are specially conceived for the clients, they are not really 'discounted', but they do represent a considerable saving over the normal cost of such menus, which would be closer to 1000 francs. The restaurants benefit by increased business during quiet periods, and, as the menu offered is both pre-set and must be reserved in advance, the restaurant knows the exact number of covers that must be produced, thus helping to reduce wastage. The experiment has been very successful, with over 1000 covers served in the first 4 months alone.

An interesting point about Groupe Degriftour's products is that they are all leisure oriented, in direct contrast with the majority of other electronic distribution channels and services. Could this be because Degriftour believe that the leisure sector will be the more important one in future?

### Innovative Distribution

In addition to offering innovative products, Degriftour are unusual in the way in which they choose to make their products available to the marketplace. As was discussed earlier, the nature of the product – last-minute availability – makes the use of normal travel distribution channels such as brochures and high street stores impossible. Instead, all distribution is carried out electronically and all sales are made directly to the customer. The channels currently used include Minitel and Telesales.

### Minitel

All of Degriftour's services are available over the Minitel network (Fig. 4.B). Launched in the early 1980s, this Videotext system quickly gained popularity as a result of a major campaign by the French government. The first 4.5 million users were simply given Minitel access terminals for free. These connect to their host computer over standard telephone lines, and allow access to over 30,000 different services, including home shopping, directory enquiries and banking services. While today the system is generally seen as being outdated, its use has helped to establish a nation-wide familiarity with interactive technology, as it forms an integral part of everyday life for both business and leisure users in France. While the system is limited by its simple text-based

**Fig. 4.B.** Degriftour over Minitel.

interface, it has the advantage of being secure, and thus payment and other security worries are not a problem.

An important feature of the Minitel system is that users pay to access most services, with the revenue being split between France Telecom and the service provider (current rates for the Degriftour are from 1.12 to 2.23 francs per minute). Thus, Degriftour benefits from two revenue sources – one from the connection fees and the other from the commissions it receives from selling travel products. However, with 5.9 million customers, each spending an average of 10 minutes shopping and booking, connection fees make up a substantial proportion of Degriftour's revenue.

### *Telesales*

Certain Degriftour services are also available over a premium rate telephone service. While this is limited to the day's special offers – Degriftour's 'Coups de Coeurs' and Reductour's 'Supers Affaires' (last-minute, last-minute availability?) – the service also generates additional revenue for the company through its connection fees.

### Degriftour and the Internet

Degriftour has naturally acted to take advantage of the opportunities offered by the World Wide Web. However, the diffusion of Internet use has not yet been as widespread in France as in other countries, in part due to the presence of the older Minitel technology. The attitude of many French people is that since the Minitel is available, is secure and it works, why should they change? The majority of Degriftour's customers are French, so it has no intention of abandoning the Minitel network just yet. As Francis Reverse, Chairman and President of Groupe Degriftour points out: 'There are about 80 million Internet surfers in the world, out of 6 billion people, i.e. 13 out of 1000. In France, Minitel users are 20 million out of 60 million French people, i.e. over 300 out of 1000!'. This gives Degriftour a compelling reason to keep using Minitel as their primary distribution media, particularly in the short run.

However, the Web will slowly gain acceptance, edged on by encouragement from the French government which does not want to see their nation left behind in an increasingly wired world. Ironically, the factor that has retarded development – the Minitel system – may eventually help in the diffusion of the Internet, as it has resulted in a general population with an above-average familiarity with IT and which is used to searching for information and buying products online. As the Minitel becomes more and more archaic, they will naturally progress to a more modern technology, and the Web looks likely to become the one chosen.

A major challenge for Degriftour will be to retain their existing customer base when they migrate from Minitel to the Web. Here they will face increased competition from the travel Mega sites (such as Internet Travel Network (ITN), Expedia and TravelWeb) which were not available over Minitel. One strategy being pursued is to form alliances with the major French Internet service providers such as AOL France, Wanadoo and Multicable, who need sites with French language content to attract local subscribers. These strategic partnerships mean that customers can be routed to the Degriftour Web sites when they connect through links from the service providers' start-up pages.

Where Degriftour sees real potential is in the ability of the Web to help to increase its business. Already, research has shown that its Web sites are attracting new customers within France, thus generating incremental revenue, rather than simply cannibalizing those customers who previously used the Minitel service. Also, as all the data on the Web sites are available in both French and English, Degriftour is beginning to gain a market share outside of France as a result of its relatively unique product offerings and focus. Degriftour has also used the Web recently to launch its first service that is not entirely aimed at the French public. 'Club Bonjour France' is focused on selling products to consumers intending to holiday in France and thus services both the domestic and the incoming tourist. Its range of product offerings is quite broad, and includes hotels, villas, gites, camping sites, theme weekends, B&Bs, cabins on riverboats and private residences. The low incremental cost of storing data means that very comprehensive descriptions can be included on the service. For example, if a hotel has a good restaurant, its menu and price are often included. The cost to be listed on the service is low (a one-off payment of 100 francs) and thus it is economical for smaller suppliers to use the system. Naturally many of these are unique, but the flexibility and limitless inexpensive storage space of the Web distribution channel allows such disparate products to be incorporated. Suppliers must, however, give an allocation of availability to be listed, and thus give Degriftour an opportunity to earn commission by selling them online.

Undoubtedly the Web will continue to grow in importance for Degriftour. Booking volumes are already growing rapidly – from 3% of their total volume in the first quarter of 1996 to 13% for the same period the following year. As Web users cannot be charged a connection fee, this will change the cost structure of the group. Already they have imposed a 100 franc booking fee on each booking processed over the Internet. The question is – will customers accept it?

# Case Study 9: TravelWeb

### www.travelweb.com

TravelWeb is an innovative Web-based system that allows customers to find information about and make bookings for hotel and airline products over the World Wide Web. Customers who wish to make their own travel arrangements can shop for their ideal product, make a secure credit card-guaranteed reservation and receive confirmation within seconds. The service is available 24 hours a day, 365 days a year, from anywhere in the world and can be accessed from any Web browser (Fig. 4.C).

Following its launch in 1994, TravelWeb quickly became one of the world's leading online hotel reservations and information systems. Airline booking capacity was added in August 1996, making it the only Web site that combined real-time direct hotel reservations capability with the ability to purchase a flight on airlines around the world. Plans are also in place to offer car hire booking facilities through a partnership with Hertz, the world's largest car rental company, which will make TravelWeb one of the most comprehensive full-featured travel site on the Internet. By offering such a broad range of travel services, TravelWeb hopes to overcome one of the problems of using the Internet – subscribers not knowing where to look for information – as TravelWeb is effectively 'a one stop shop for all travel information and reservations'. Perhaps the best indicator of its success in achieving this is shown by its sales. In the first year of operations, sales increased by an average of approximately 40% each month and it is now processing approximately $1 million worth of reservations each month.

The range of products available over TravelWeb is phenomenal – over 24,000 hotel properties in more than 150 countries worldwide, including 90 different hotel chain brands; and flights on more than 300 airlines. Altavista maintains that there are over 10,000 other Internet sites with hyperlinks to TravelWeb. On average, about 33,000 people access the site each day and reservations have been received from 29 countries, attesting to the global reach of the system. Although expectations were that upscale business-orientated hotels would generate the most interest, experience has shown that this is not the case, and booking levels seem to vary proportionately with the number of properties that a chain lists.

This case study was prepared by Peter O'Connor, Assistant Professor, Institut de Management Hôtelier International (IMHI), as a basis for discussion rather than to illustrate either effective or ineffective handling of an administrative problem.
All rights reserved.

**Fig. 4.C.** The TravelWeb home page.

## Pegasus Systems Inc.

The success of TravelWeb cannot be discussed in isolation. TravelWeb is a subsidiary of Dallas-based Pegasus Systems Inc., a holding company set up in 1995 as the parent company of three established and successful technology-based services: TravelWeb, THISCo and the Hotel Clearing Corporation (HCC). The synergy that is provided by this portfolio of three companies makes Pegasus a powerful force in travel electronic distribution.

The origins of the Pegasus Corporation lie in THISCo, which was set up in 1989 to design and operate a computerized switch that would simplify the connection of hotel CRSs to the GDS (Box 4.A). Hotel companies were spending approximately $0.5 million each to develop direct interfaces between their CRS and each of the major GDSs and, despite the level of expenditure, the resulting interface was still quite basic. In an attempt to overcome this problem, 15 of the major players in the international hotel industry, many of them direct competitors, began cooperating in 1994 by establishing THISCo. The company's first service (UltraSwitch) in effect acted as a gateway between the GDS and any hotel CRS. As a result, hotel companies only had to develop a single interface, from their in-house system to the Switch, to connect to all the GDSs. The product has been very successful and currently links over 27,000 hotels from 128 chains with the four major GDSs and a variety of other regional CRSs. Travel agent bookings are encouraged by the services of another Pegasus company, the HCC. This monitors and tracks the bookings flowing through the THISCo system, and helps to ensure that travel agents are paid the resulting commissions. This has encouraged travel agents to book electronically, and has helped THISCo to achieve one of its major objectives: to significantly increase the number of hotel rooms booked through the GDS.

However, the disadvantage of the GDS route is its transaction cost. In addition to the travel agent commission, the GDS service provider

---

**Box 4.A.** The original THISCo partners.

| | | |
|---|---|---|
| Anasazi Inc. | Hilton Corporation | Marriott Hotels |
| Best Western Hotels | Hyatt Hotels | Promus Hotels |
| Choice Hotels | Inter-Continental Hotels | Read Travel Group |
| Forte Hotels | ITT Sheraton | Utell International |
| HFS Inc. | La Quinta Inns | Westin Hotels and Resorts |

typically takes a fixed fee for processing the booking, and THISCo also adds a smaller fee for the use of its switching facilities. All in all, these distribution costs can eat away a significant proportion of the revenue from the sale. For that reason, a new service known as 'TravelWeb' was introduced in 1994. This is linked electronically to THISCo, but bypasses the GDS/travel agent route by accessing the customer directly over the World Wide Web. In effect, TravelWeb provides its member properties with 'complete electronic brochure facilities' which allow potential customers to see not only room rates and descriptions but also images of rooms, restaurants, meeting facilities, local recreation activities, maps and more. Two of the original THISCo partners (Hyatt and Best Western) were the first companies to experiment with distributing information about their product in this way. Initial reactions were very good. For example, Best Western initially listed information about 150 of their hotels. In the first 2 weeks, these pages were accessed 79,000 times. According to industry experts, a conversion rate of only 10% would mean that their investment would have repaid itself in the first month. In addition to lower capital costs, distribution through TravelWeb also has a lower transaction cost, as THISCo only charge $0.23 for reservations flowing through the World Wide Web compared with the average of $3.50 currently being charged by the major GDS.

### How TravelWeb Works

Visitors to TravelWeb are presented with a complete electronic travel brochure that they can browse to find and book hotels or airline flights that interest them. Pre-registration is not required and, unlike many other travel-related Web sites, users all over the world can use the site for booking purposes, simply by guaranteeing their reservation using a credit card. Comprehensive search facilities are provided, and users can locate suitable hotels by geographical location, chain name, rate range and amenities/facilities. The system will list the matching hotels, and allow the user to read descriptions and view pictures of the rooms, restaurants, meeting facilities and local recreational activities associated with each property. Once a choice has been made, the link with THISCo allows up-to-date rates/availability to be displayed and online reservations to be made. At this stage, the system collects essential data such as the user's name and credit card details, and processes the reservation. A confirmation number is provided while the user is still online, and this is followed up with an Email reconfirming the details after a few minutes as a security precaution. Users can also view previous reservations that they made through TravelWeb and can cancel reservations made over the site if necessary. All of these transactions flow across the Internet, through TravelWeb to THISCo and ultimately to the hotel companies' CRS (Fig. 4.D).

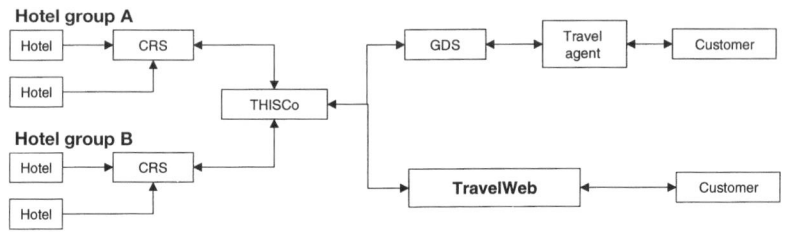

**Fig. 4.D.** Hotel distribution over TravelWeb.

Given the large number of properties represented by TravelWeb, it would obviously be very difficult to design, manage and maintain individual Web pages for each one. Instead, property details are maintained in a vast database, and HTML pages are generated on the fly using CGI in response to user requests. These pages follow a standard template, displaying relatively basic information such as facilities and rates, as well as the closest airport and a single graphic. One of the criticisms of this approach is that the potential for marketing through differentiation is limited as, in effect, all pages have the same appearance. However, an alternative opinion is that this standardization is, in fact, an advantage, as users know exactly where to find the information they require on the page. It thus permits easy comparison of different properties, as similar information is always in the same position. Many hotel companies also maintain their own Web sites, with their own individual look for marketing purposes, but link back into TravelWeb for booking purposes.

### TravelWeb's Customer Focus

The success of TravelWeb can be explained in part by two factors: their constant culture of innovation and their focus on the customer. These two considerations have combined to help ensure that the TravelWeb site is constantly developing and enhancing its services to better serve the user. For example, the range and quality of information provided is continually being expanded. In addition to descriptions, rate and availability information for each individual hotel, interactive site maps allow the user to view the location of the property and give directions to help travellers find it. Up-to-date weather reports and forecasts are also available on the site, and a resort-focused interactive travel magazine known as 'Travelscape' has recently been added. This has been seamlessly woven into the site, providing articles on the world's top destinations along with helpful travel tips. These new features help users to do their entire trip planning without ever having to leave the site – which helps to explain why it was nominated by *Fortune Magazine* as the 'best listing of hotels around the world'.

Similarly, customer's concerns about online bookings have also been addressed. The absence of user logins and passwords and the incorporation of powerful search engines that help to locate appropriate products minimize online search times. Security worries are allayed by the use of Netscape's *Secure Sockets Layer* encryption technology to protect credit card transactions. In addition, all bookings are confirmed by Email to help prevent fraudulent transactions. Airline booking facilities have recently been enhanced by an agreement with ITN. In addition to being faster and easier to use, the new reservations engine provides features such as lowest fare searching, seat selection, local currency pricing, worldwide ticket delivery and instant confirmation from more than 300 airlines around the world. The ability to distribute special offers was also included with the launch of 'Click-it! Weekends' at the end of 1996. This service lists last-minute hotel availability, offering low rates for the weekend following, thus helping hotels to dispose of distressed inventory while also allowing users to find a bargain.

TravelWeb has also enhanced its services to its hotel company clients. For example, it has rapidly expanded its client audience (and thus the potential number of bookings for hotels) using strategic alliances with other Web-based travel services. For example, during 1997, it signed agreements with Preview Travel (which has 850,000 registered users on America On-Line), ITN and Microsoft Expedia allowing each of these services use of TravelWeb's unique booking engine and access to all of the hotels listed on TravelWeb. The company sees itself as being in the reservation transaction processing business, and has developed a product which allows them to provide this service to other companies much more cheaply and more efficiently than developing it for themselves. TravelWeb receives a transaction fee in return, the hotels get more bookings and the entire process is invisible to the user.

# Case Study 10: Microsoft Expedia

### www.expedia.com

Microsoft Expedia is a convenient, comprehensive travel site offering real-time travel planning and purchasing information on the World Wide Web (Fig. 4.E). It offers an integrated set of travel information and booking services that helps users to choose where they want to go, shop for the best prices and book their air, car and hotel reservations. Launched in October 1996, it represents the first attempt of a major non-travel industry company to exploit the developing online travel services market.

By tapping into the same reservation systems used by travel professionals, supplementing it with information from a variety of other sources, and displaying its results in an easy-to-understand way,

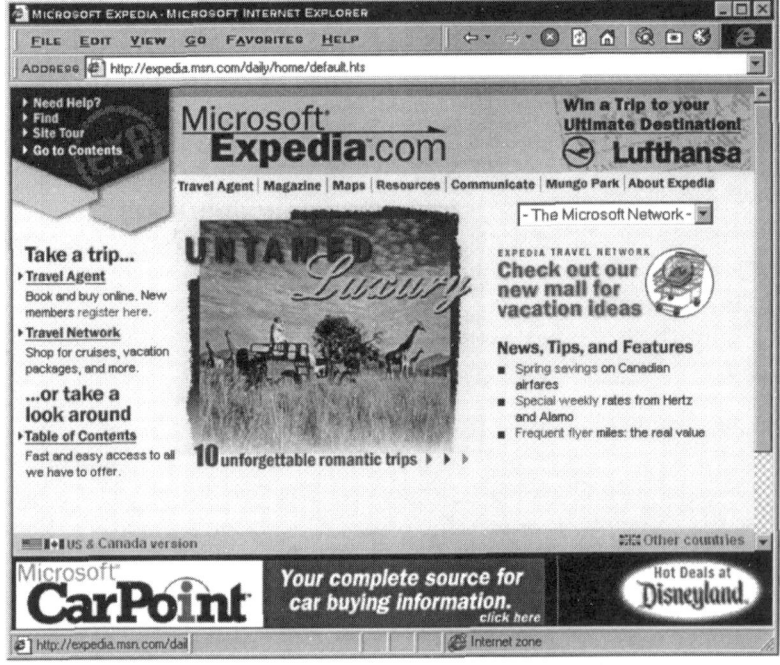

**Fig. 4.E.** Microsoft Expedia's home page.

Expedia allows users to shop for the best fares and schedules. Innovative features include a series of software 'wizards' to guide users through the searching and booking process, and the ability to build up a complete personalized itinerary including air, hotel and car reservations.

### The Microsoft Corporation

The Microsoft Corporation is the world leader in the provision of software for PCs. Founded by Bill Gates in 1975, the company offers a wide range of products and services for business and personal use, each designed with the mission of making it easier and more enjoyable for people to take advantage of the power of technology in their everyday lives. As such, Expedia fits in well with Microsoft's philosophy. According to Bill Gates (Chairman and CEO of Microsoft):

> Expedia builds on Microsoft's commitment to using the Internet to solve real customer needs. Providing people with real-time access to constantly changing information in an easy-to-use way furthers our longstanding vision that the personal computer is the ultimate information tool for consumers. Being able to tap into and book the latest, lowest airfares right from your PC with Expedia is very compelling. We think it will reshape the way consumers plan and purchase their travel.

Microsoft hopes that its combination of experience in consumer software and the provision of in-depth multimedia content will help to make Expedia the premier site for planning and purchasing travel on the Web. According to John Neilson, Vice President, Information Business Unit at Microsoft:

> Our goal with Expedia is to provide travellers with all the information they need to take a trip – from exploring destinations to making reservations to actually purchasing tickets. Not only does Expedia give travellers up-to-the-minute information on fares, schedules and accommodation, they can also explore their destinations online before they get there, thus helping them to select the options that best meet their travel needs.

### Expedia Travel Services

The first time a user accesses Expedia (specifically the *Travel Agent* section, which permits booking), they must register with the service by creating a user profile. This provides Expedia with demographic data, and information on travel preferences such as preferred seat, special meal requirements, etc. This is then stored as a 'cookie' on the user's hard disk, which is used by Expedia to recognize the user on subsequent visits. (Users can also access the system from other computers by entering a username and password.) Once users have registered, they then have access to all of Expedia's services including the following.

**1.** *Expedia Travel Agent.* This is the heart of Expedia, and allows users to access the same database that travel agents use to check availability and make bookings, without all the confusing codes and jargon. Software wizards – a series of prompts and questions – guide the user through the process of researching, booking and purchasing. For airline and car hire bookings, these invisibly transform the customer's requests into the correct format for submission to Worldspan, thus permitting reservations to be made with most of the major airlines and car rental companies. Hotel bookings, on the other hand, are processed through TravelWeb, as will be discussed below. Innovative features of the service include 'Seat Pinpointer', which allows users to select their preferred seat on a graphical map of their airplane, and 'Fare Compare', which allows users to compare competing fares by producing a table-like screen displaying each of the fares and any restrictions that apply.

Tickets can be paid for online using a credit card or, if users prefer, they can call a toll-free telephone number to enter their card details the first time they use the service. These details can then be stored (in encrypted format) as part of their user profile for use in future bookings. All data being transmitted over the Web is protected using Secure Socket Layer encryption, and the system automatically validates the credit card number, owner's name, billing address and credit limit before the transaction is finalized. Reservations are confirmed immediately, and Expedia also sends an Email message to confirm the transaction. Tickets can be sent by mail, express mail, or they can be picked up at the airport ticket counter. Expedia also supports the developing 'e-ticket' technology that allows customers to travel without a physical ticket.

**2.** *Expedia Hotel Directory.* This features more than 25,000 hotel properties and 5000 B&Bs around the world, with information on rates, amenities and more. In addition to pictures and descriptions, Expedia can plot the hotel location on a city map, thus helping travellers to be sure their choice is conveniently located (Fig. 4.F). Since June 1998, hotel reservations are processed through a strategic partnership with Pegasus's TravelWeb, with Expedia seamlessly making use of TravelWeb's hotel booking engine.

**3.** *Expedia Fare Tracker.* This personalized service keeps travellers

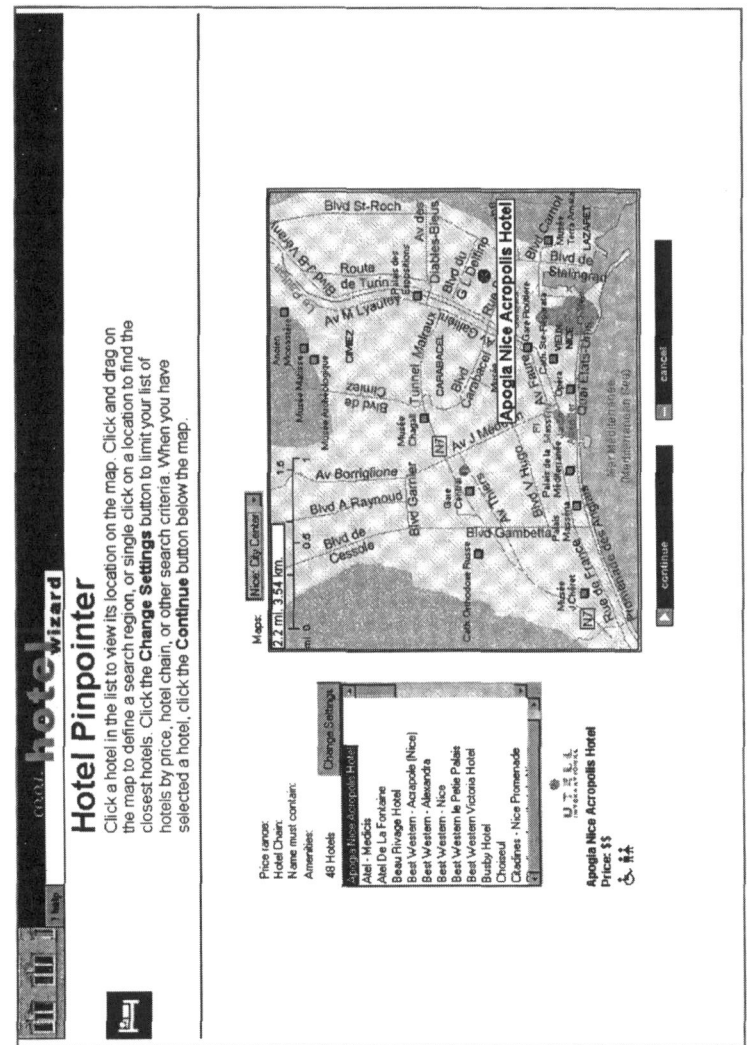

**Fig. 4.F.** Expedia's Hotel Pinpointer screen.

informed of the best airfares between two cities of their choosing. Users can select up to three pairs of cities, and Expedia will monitor the GDS and send them periodic Emails highlighting the best fares available between these destinations.

**4.** *Expedia World Guide.* This guidebook-style service includes cultural, historical and entertainment information on more than 330 destinations worldwide. It includes thousands of photos, and provides suggestions on what a user might like to see and do if they visit a featured destination.

**5.** *Expedia Travel Community.* This acts as a form of interactive bulletin board, allowing users to post questions and share travel tips with fellow travellers. Travel experts serve as forum managers, and can be contacted in a live question and answer setting.

Expedia also operates a range of other services, all aimed at increasing customer service and enhancing the travel experience. For example, its 'Flight Info' feature allows users to see real-time flight information so that they can check on the status of their flight before they leave for the airport. 'Expedia Magazine' includes breaking travel news, feature articles, weather reports and information such as currency exchange rates. (At some point, members may get 'personal travel news' geared to their stated and actual preferences, or even have a personalized home page on the site containing information personally geared to them.) Expedia also offers toll-free telephone and Email support to customers who need to change their travel plans or experience a travel emergency. This support facility is staffed by experienced travel professionals and is available 24 hours a day, 7 days a week.

### Future Directions

Despite not being the first, Expedia is the leader in terms of revenues and, because of Microsoft's resources, brand equity and expertise in technology, is seen as being the one to watch in a very competitive field. According to Eric Blatchford, Product Manager Travel: 'Microsoft sees three parts in the equation for Expedia's success: great technology, great editorial and great service, and we intend to deliver on all three'. In addition, Microsoft's experience in creating smart and useful software gives it a major advantage that sets it apart from the other online travel services.

Despite projections to the contrary, Expedia is making money. By February 1997, the service was selling more than $1 million worth of reservations per week, putting it well into the top 40 travel agencies worldwide. Approximately 50,000 users a day access the service, and revenues are steadily climbing towards the $2 million per week mark. The site has won numerous Web and press awards (including *PC Magazine*'s 'Top 100 Web Sites', *PC Week*'s 'Top Electronic Commerce Site' and *USA Today*'s '4-Star Web Site'). It also has a very high customer satisfaction ratio, with '87% of customers very or extremely likely to purchase air tickets again'.

In typical Microsoft fashion, Expedia is gradually evolving (to date there have been three major upgrades), incorporating the best features of their competitors and innovative ideas from other companies. However, the next priority for Expedia must be to increase the number of transactions over the system to take maximum advantage of its investment. Some of the strategies being used include broadening the product line by including tours, packages and cruises on the system, and expanding the system geographically. To date, Expedia has focused mainly on the US and Canadian markets, but is now making itself available to European customers. It does, however, recognize that travel needs and purchasing behaviour are not the same all over the world, and thus is forming partnerships with agencies in targeted countries to help bring a local flavour to its products and services.

Another strategy being pursued to help increase the volume of transactions is to provide its expertise in online selling to other companies. For example, Microsoft Travel Technologies has cooperated with American Express in the development of American Express Interactive (AXI), an Internet-based service aimed at servicing and managing corporate travel. It has also provided the booking technology for both Northwest and Continental Airline's Web sites. Such alliances are important as more people are realizing that it is impossible to provide world class service in every aspect of the travel distribution chain. Instead the companies that will be successful are those that can form non-exclusive alliances with other companies, each of which is outstanding at its own job and can successfully combine their own expertise with services bought in from other industry leaders.

# Chapter 5

# What Next?

Poon, in her landmark book *Tourism, Technology and Competitive Advantage* (Poon, 1993), makes the point that it is not a single technology (such as computers or telephones or videotext) that is being diffused throughout the tourism sector, but an entire system of these technologies. In addition, technology is not being used by just airlines or hotels or travel agents, but by all of them. Advances in the application of developing technologies to the tourism sector are also happening at a rapid pace. For example, approximately 1 year ago, when this text was conceived, it was envisaged that this last chapter would discuss the use of CD-ROMs and multimedia kiosks, as, at the time, these seemed to have the greatest potential as developing tourism technologies. However, these topics seem to have failed to capture the imagination of the tourism industry, and, to some extent, have been overtaken by the pace of technology. While they are still important, entirely different and exciting subjects now suggest themselves. Therefore, while reading this chapter, please remember the quandary of the technology author trying to forecast the future – the only thing that is certain is uncertainty. The technologies and systems mentioned here may succeed or may sink into oblivion. All that can be said for certain is that they seemed like a good idea at the time.

## 5.1 Global Distribution Systems Revisited

As we have seen, the GDSs have traditionally enjoyed an enviable position within the travel distribution chain. Their key role as information brokers made their systems an essential tool for travel agents, allowing them to collect commission on the millions of travel transactions made each year. In addition, because of their penetration into the travel agency market, many other electronic distribution systems interfaced with them, paying them a fee for each transaction processed, thus adding further to their profitability. However, as has been discussed in previous chapters, the GDSs suffer from several limitations. Their restrictive database structure makes them less suitable for the distribution of travel products other than airline seats; their textual user interface now looks old and tired, and has to a large extent been superceded by newer graphic user-interfaced technology; and increased competition in the global marketplace has caused tourism suppliers to question the high cost of distributing over the traditional GDS-to-travel agent route. As a result, the GDSs are under threat of disintermediation from newer distribution channels such as the Internet, which offer a direct route to the customer.

Obviously the GDSs are reacting to these challenges. Since the beginning of the 1990s, each has undertaken massive renovations and enhancements of their hotel and car hire modules, with the goal of improving the marketability and accuracy of the data displayed on the travel agent's terminal (Table 5.1). Restrictions in terms of the number of rates and the scope of the descriptions that can be displayed have been considerably lessened. For example, room types and rates are now associated with each other and all of the major systems now also allow the sale of negotiated rates. Hotels have traditionally offered these special rates to their high-volume corporate customers, but until comparatively recently travel agents could not use their GDS terminals to reserve them. Both the hotel and the chain descriptions have been expanded and restructured, allowing much more of the character and capabilities of each hotel to be communicated and making it easier for travel agents to find the information that they need (Schmid, 1994).

The GDSs are also striving to take advantage of the opportunities presented by new technology (Wolff, 1996a). Recognizing that many tourism suppliers wish to reduce their costs of distribution by bypassing travel agents, and not wishing to be caught in this disintermediation, many are introducing direct-to-consumer routes such as dial-up access and World Wide Web sites. A good example of the dial-up strategy is United Airlines 'Connection' product. Software is sent by mail to selected customers who install the program on their PC. After dialling into the Connection database, they can check arrival and departure times, access frequent flyer mileage accounts and, most importantly, get interactive booking access to the CRS, in this case, Galileo International through Apollo (Odell, 1996). Other airlines have similar schemes, but United's is slightly different in that it is only available to 'elite' passengers – those who travel more than 30,000 miles a year on the carrier. While these people only represent a small percentage of their customer base, they generate a disproportionate

**Table 5.1.** GDS feature cross-reference table. Source: adapted and updated from Emmer and Tauck (1993).

| Feature (generic name) | Galileo International | SABRE | Amadeus/System One | WORLDSPAN |
|---|---|---|---|---|
| Type A link | Inside Link | Direct Connect | Complete Access | Access Plus |
| Seamless connectivity | Inside Availability | Direct Connect Availability | Complete Access Plus | Hotel Source |
| Hotel program | Room Master | Shaarp Plus | Amadeus Hotels | Hotel Select |
| Negotiated rate program | Multi-level Rates | Multi-tiered Rates | Negotiated Rates | Secured Rates |
| Sign-on advertising | Front Page News | Sine In Message | Sign In Message | PrimeSINE |
| System news page | TD/NEWS, Headlines | System HOT Messages | HOT News, Bulletins | Associate Marketplace |
| Visual imaging product | Spectrum | SABREVision | | |

amount of the carrier's revenue, thus justifying the investment in developing and operating the scheme.

The second method of reaching customers directly is exemplified by UK independent airline British Midland, who were the first to offer interactive flight reservations on the Web (Odell, 1996). Instead of requiring special software, the airline allows customers to check availability and reserve seats on their Web site (www.iflybritishmidland.com) using a standard Web browser and paying with a credit card. Being a small carrier, they felt that they were not gaining any advantage from the use of traditional GDS distribution, and thus decided to widen their accessibility to include the maximum number of channels. Although the economics of such a strategy have not yet proved themselves, a variety of other airlines (particularly smaller, budget airlines such as Alaskan Airways and SouthWest Airways) have followed suit and introduced similar Web booking facilities.

The major GDSs have also joined in the stampede to get online and some time ago introduced their own dial-up products (such as EasySABRE or Worldspan's Travel Shopper) and are now experimenting with distribution over the Internet. Most, with the notable exception of Galileo International, have launched their own Web sites, providing information and reservations functions, as can be seen from Table 5.1. However, while the GDS companies have extensive experience in the provision of travel information, their marketing skills are relatively weak. To overcome this, many have also chosen to form partnerships with other companies to develop powerful brands (Table 5.2). Sites developed as a result of such alliances, such as Travelocity (powered by SABRE) or Microsoft Expedia (developed jointly by Worldspan and Microsoft), are among the most successful on the Web. Another strategy being pursued by the GDS is to provide technology to support travel agencies wishing to set up Web sites with online

**Table 5.2.** GDS Internet-based products.

| System | Branded Web site | Travel agency reservations engine | Corporate product |
| --- | --- | --- | --- |
| SABRE | Travelocity | SABRE Web Reservations | Business Travel Solutions |
| Worldspan | Expedia | Worldspan Wave | Trip Manager |
| Galileo | — | Travelpoint | (No name) International |
| Amadeus | Amadeus.net | Amadeus.net | Corporate Traveller |

booking facilities. Most of the GDSs see the travel agent as their primary customer, and thus wish to strengthen their mutually beneficial relationship (French, 1998). As a result, they have developed products (such as SABRE's 'Web Reservations' or Amadeus's 'Amadeus.net' that can be incorporated by travel agents into their own 'private label' web sites. Reservations made through the sites are routed through their respective travel agency and earn commission in the same way as 'normal' GDS reservations. This provides agents with a valuable facility that complements and allows them to grow their business.

Thus, as can be seen from Fig. 5.1, the data stored on the GDS database are no longer just available to travel agents, but are also now being distributed directly to the public over a wide variety of direct channels. The limiting factor in the widespread acceptance and use of these direct channels is, however, the need to issue tickets for airline flights. While domestic flights are not affected (and indeed electronic ticketing is being widely used within the large US market), airlines must by law make passengers aware of their conditions of carriage on international flights under the terms of the Warsaw Convention. In the past, the accepted way of doing this was to use printed paper tickets issued by a travel agent. At the moment, trials are underway to develop viable electronic alternatives. These include British Airways' E-Ticket, which uses the magnetic strip from a credit card to identify the passenger, and Lufthansa's ChipCard, which is a smart-card issued to frequent flyers and contains a chip which can store flight details. However, until there is general acceptance of an international standard, electronic ticketing is not going to become commonplace and open the floodgates for the mainstream sale of airline seats over direct channels.

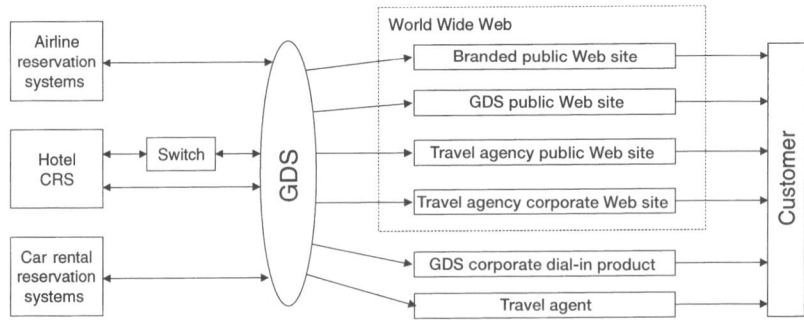

**Fig. 5.1.** The new GDS distribution environment.

## 5.2 Hard Storage Devices

There has been a variety of experiments with the production of hard storage-based promotional tools that can be given to consumers for use at their own convenience. These usually take the form of compact disks (such as CD-ROM or CD-*i*), although floppy disk-based examples, which can either be run directly or be uncompressed on to the user hard disk, have also been produced in the past. However, volume restricts the amount of data that can be stored in this way, and thus such products tend to be limited in scope. The larger storage capacity of CDs allows vast amounts of multimedia information, complete with colour pictures, sounds and video clips to be incorporated into an interactive brochure that can be used on the consumer's home or office computer (Pollock, 1995b). CDs are easy and cheap to produce and distribute, and the equipment needed to play them (along with the other devices needed to view multimedia presentations such as sound cards) has become nearly ubiquitous on modern PCs (Schaeffer, 1994).

CD-ROM-based products can be focused on either the intermediary or the end consumer. For example, American Airlines teamed up with the Reed Travel Group to produce the Jaguar Electronic Hotel Directory, which was designed to be used by travel agents alongside the SABRE booking system, where it became known as SABREVision (Heinzemann, 1994). This allowed travel agents to call up pictures, digital maps and very detailed information on each of the featured properties, and then check availability/rates and subsequently make a booking on their SABRE terminal. It was a highly successful sales tool that allowed travel agents to sell hotels to their customers more effectively, with agencies using it doubling or even tripling their previous number of hotel bookings (Vlitos-Rowe, 1992). Groupe Accor, on the other hand, regularly produces a CD-ROM containing information about and pictures of their hotels worldwide. This is more focused on the consumer, and allows them to search for properties geographically or using a list of desired facilities. To make a booking, the user can contact the hotel directly or can telephone one of Accor's telesales centres throughout the world.

Developing devices, such as digital versatile disks (DVDs) will expand storage capability even further, allowing vast amounts of video and other information to be distributed if desired. 'DK Eyewitness World Atlas' provides an extremely good example of what is possible using this technology. This allows users to fly around the world, choosing their own height, speed and direction, and displays real (as opposed to computer-generated) satellite images of the landscape underneath. As well as the 3-D maps, the DVD also contains a wealth of other information. This includes a 2-D reference atlas (with hyperlinks to a selection of the best Web sites on a particular country or region), a slide show of high-quality photographs, short videos on attractions, a spinning globe showing political and physical information and even satellite pictures of the world at night, all contained on a tiny 4 inch disk (Sykes, 1998).

However, the potential of hard storage is limited because of the difficulty in keeping its data up to date. Even if, as is the case with newer versions of CD-ROMs, the storage device is not read only, the lack of a communications link means that the information cannot easily be updated. Thus, while this technology has the advantage of volume storage in a small, lightweight format, they are in reality little better than digital versions of the old paper-based brochures and guides. As a result, they have, to a large extent, been superceded by technologies such as the Internet that permit cheap, fast access to more up-to-date information.

## 5.3 Multimedia Kiosks

While hard storage forms of electronic brochures are generally sent to customers for use on their own computers, sometimes it makes sense to bring the customer to the storage device. Increasingly electronic brochures are being housed in self-service kiosks located in areas that experience large volumes of visitors, such as in hotel lobbies, outside tourist attractions, at airports and other transportation centres or even on screens at the back of airline seats. These can be operated by either commercial or government organizations. In the former case, tourism suppliers pay a fee to be included on the service, and thus not every hotel, restaurant or attraction in an area is likely to be included. Where kiosks are operated by RTOs, they are more likely to be exhaustive in their information content, and are also perceived to provide more impartial information than the commercially driven systems (Kingsley and Fesenmaier, 1995).

Most kiosks are based on PCs, enclosed in a case for protection. Touch-screen technology is now relatively standard as it allows the use of a Web-like hypertext interface to browse through its information. Most kiosks also include multimedia facilities such as the ability to play sounds and display video, which helps to enrich the selling experience and, since all the data are being drawn off the disk of the kiosk, there are no bandwidth or performance limitations that could delay the display of the presentation. A typical session might start with the kiosk displaying a map of the area divided into four or five sections. Users can then select the region they wish to inquire about, and a menu of the features in the selected area appears on screen. Users can select a category (such as hotels or restaurants), and then scroll through the various listings and advertisements included in the database. Most systems are also capable of printing information pages, direction maps or other promotional material that the user can take away with them (Kingsley and Fesenmaier, 1995). Where the kiosk is networked to (for example) a destination management system or other electronic distribution channel, dynamic data such as availability and rates can also be displayed on the system. This would allow the kiosk to process inquires and reservations, with payment being accepted via a credit card reader.

## 5.4 Intranets and Extranets

While the World Wide Web has received a lot of attention in relation to its effect on tourism distribution, another set of Internet-based technologies, known as Intranets and Extranets, may have an even greater effect in the future, particularly on the highly profitable corporate travel segment. Both Intranets and Extranets use the same communications media, protocols and browsers as the Web, but are differentiated by both ownership and by closed user-group features (Pollock, 1997a). Intranets are generally owned and operated by a single organization and are essentially private in that they only permit users from within that organization to access their pages. Such users may be located within a single building, or may be situated on opposite sides of the world, but only specifically nominated people can access the system. When the scope of the system is expanded and the nominees include users from outside the organization, such as suppliers or customers, the system is generally known as an Extranet.

Intranets and Extranets have the potential to replace proprietary transaction-processing systems both within and between companies, as they are cheaper to set up, easier to use and are platform independent. In addition, because they are only open to selected users, they are more secure and more consistent in terms of speed than the more public Internet (Edwards *et al.*, 1998). As a result, they are more suitable for electronic commerce transactions, and are increasingly being implemented to facilitate business-to-business transactions in a variety of industries (Moran, 1997). Travel companies have an opportunity to benefit from these developments by building partnerships with appropriate companies and including pages on their Intranets. According to American Express, travel and travel-related costs are the third largest controllable expense in most large companies, after payroll and maintenance of capital assets. However, such travel expenditure has traditionally been decentralized and unmanaged, resulting in a single company using multiple travel agencies for reservation purposes. This makes it almost impossible for companies to use their purchasing power to obtain discounts on travel services (Arthur Andersen, 1998). Although many companies have developed formal corporate policies to help reduce this problem, in practice these are difficult to implement and control (Vlitos-Rowe, 1995).

Internet/Extranet technology can help by linking the company directly to a nominated or preferred travel agency, through which all travel bookings must be made. Within the company's Intranet, when the employee clicks on travel, they are taken directly to the partner agency's page, into which they enter details of the travel services they require. This request is then sent electronically for authorization by the appropriate people, and then forwarded for processing to the travel agency, thus helping to further streamline the process and reduce costs (Bloch *et al.*, 1996b). Formal corporate travel policies (such as, for example, that everyone must fly economy on trips under 300 miles) can be incorporated into the system, and, as all bookings are made through a single agency, the company is able to negotiate volume discounts or commission sharing (Bloch and Segev, 1997). Most systems can also automatically electronically bill the company's accounting department when the tickets have been issued, and provide a variety of management information to help the company manage their travel budget more effectively (Manente *et al.*, 1998). The fact that all the data are entered by the user, that all documents flow electronically, that corporate travel policies are automatically enforced and that management information is automatically compiled leads to real quantifiable savings, which some analysts have estimated to be in the region of $30–40 per ticket (Arthur Andersen, 1998).

The Web Travel Mega systems have been quick to spot this opportunity and are ideally positioned to exploit it, given their experience with both Internet technology and travel distribution. For example, Internet Travel Network has launched a product known as Internet Travel Manager (ITM), which facilitates corporate booking and travel management services over either the Internet or a corporate Intranet. Similarly, Microsoft and American Express have teamed up to develop AXI, which allows users to book flights, hotels and car hire, and also integrates with American Express's 'RoundTrip' travel management product. As such systems become more commonplace, the travel agent's position in this scenario will be increasingly hard to justify. Even today, many of these systems are capable of contacting supplier's systems directly and making bookings without using the services of a travel agency. Printing tickets will become less important as the trend towards ticket-less travel expands, as all that will be needed are the confirmation numbers returned by the system. Many tourism suppliers, including hotels, car hire companies and RTOs are already experimenting by allowing tour operators, meeting planners and large corporations to access travel information and make their bookings directly over Extranets (Christensen, 1998). A leading example of such a company is Marriott International, who, instead of trying to gain exposure on the increasingly crowded Web marketplace, has instead opted to concentrate on developing pages on the Intranets of large corporations that have traditionally been their key clients. By making it easier for employees in such companies to book Marriott, they are in effect 'locking in' such business and ensuring continued bookings in the future. The economics of such a strategy are hard to beat. The Extranet channel bypasses the traditional GDS/travel agent route, and thus saves the company both a commission and a transaction charge – a saving that can be shared with the client company in the form of a better negotiated rate.

## 5.5 Home Shopping and Interactive Television

The idea of shopping from home is not new, but it has yet to gain widespread acceptance. Part of the problem lies not in the technology but in the habits of consumers. People like to go out to shop, as it is in essence a social experience, and they like to compare products in terms of quality, colour and price. While this is true of 'hard goods', with travel products and services the situation is rather different. As has already been discussed, the only way that travel products can be compared before purchase is by way of information, which can just as easily be consumed in the home (Bennett, 1998). Indeed, in many cases, this is preferable, as time is required to read and digest the data and possibly discuss it with family members. (The practice of taking home brochures from travel firms is testimony to this preference.) The increased information richness that multimedia electronic channels could bring to this equation increases the attractiveness of home shopping for travel products even more.

A variety of trials are under way throughout the world to find appropriate devices that could act as the technology for home shopping. For example, Barclay's Bank in the UK is currently experimenting with a 'screen phone' – basically a larger version of a normal phone with an in-built $8 \times 5$ cm screen. Data are transmitted over a standard phone line, and the device is being marketed as a way for customers to access their account details as well as do home shopping (Financial Times Service, 1998). However, actually achieving an acceptable level of diffusion with such devices is relatively difficult. Consumers are, for the most part, conservative in relation to the adoption of new technology. Most adopt a 'wait and see' approach, not investing in new consumer devices until a particular one has been adopted as the industry standard (Bloch *et al.*, 1996a).

Two technologies that already have widespread acceptance in the home are the television and the telephone, and the race is now on to link them into an appropriate medium for electronic commerce. While there are still a number of issues to be worked out before it becomes widespread (such as the role of the television, telephone and cable companies, the amount of bandwidth necessary to handle multimedia and video on demand, and various payment issues) interactive television is forecast to become an important channel of distribution over the next 5 years (Pollock, 1995). Experiments are currently under way in many parts of the world. For example, BT Interactive TV was piloted on selected residents of East Anglia in the UK during 1995. During this trial, travel emerged as the most popular product sold over the system, with the Thomas Cook Group offering flights, packages and a range of ancillary travel services on the system (Bennett, 1996).

At present, the capabilities of interactive television are relatively limited. Most 'broadcasters' are providing selected services such as video-on-demand and basic home shopping facilities. Others are starting to experiment with 'time-shifted' programming – showing the same news bulletin at 15 minute intervals so that if you missed it at 7 p.m., you could see it starting at 7.15 p.m. on another channel (Wingfield, 1998). However, a more elaborate vision is foreseen for the future. Imagine watching a news broadcast or a movie, and noticing an interesting product as part of the transmission. Imagine being able to pause or rewind the show, and click on the product to find out more about it, how much it costs or even purchase it there and then, and have it delivered next day! Such facilities would change advertising from being an intrusive commercial message that interrupts a person's media experience into an invited conversation with the customer. Instead of being a half-page spread in a glossy magazine that can be skipped with the flip of a page, it becomes part and parcel of the programme with which the person is interacting, ready to be peeled back like an onion with 'tell-me-more' and 'show-me-more' buttons allowing the viewer to specify exactly what information they want to see (Murphy *et al.*, 1996a).

Undoubtedly, home shopping, through whatever medium, will become more common as consumers become increasingly familiar with technology. However, the complexity of the travel product could be the key factor in determining whether a travel product can be sold successfully over this type of channel. Where the product is relatively simple (such as a domestic flight or a package holiday), consumers should feel comfortable with booking it electronically for themselves. However, where the travel experience is more complicated, most people agree that consumers will continue to seek advice and assistance from travel agents or other travel professionals.

## 5.6 Intelligent Agents

One of the problems associated with all of these developing distribution channels is that they greatly increase the amount of information that is available to the consumer. Given that we already suffer from 'information overload', providing even more data makes it more difficult, rather than easier for the consumer to find the most appropriate travel product. An experimental technology, known as *intelligent agents*, could help to navigate through this sea of data more easily.

Intelligent agents can best be described as software programs that act as electronic or virtual secretaries, working diligently on behalf of their user. Their purpose is to act as a surrogate, wading at electronic speeds through the above-mentioned flood of data (Steiner and Dufour, 1998). They normally possess an enormous amount of information about the person that they serve, and that person's preferences, relationships and obligations are interwoven into every task and decision that the agent makes. Initially, the user will have to enter most of the information to guide the task and decision-making processes. However, eventually, through the use of artificial intelligence, the agent will learn from the actions of the user about his likes and preferences and will be capable of making decisions on its own. In the future, agents will be linked over a more advanced version of today's Internet to other individual's agents, and also to agents representing suppliers and social organizations. Decisions about purchasing products will be taken by agents communicating with each other to find the best match between an individual's preferences and the products and services available (Olsen, 1997).

In relation to travel distribution, a scenario has been proposed whereby a series of intelligent agents could be used within the Internet environment to collect, collate, filter and automate the travel booking process. *Intelligent search agents* could be programmed to search the 'information superhighway' for required travel data and return the appropriate responses to the user. *Filtering agents* could be tasked to filter information from the search agents, and also to monitor push channels for other data of relevance. *Service agents* would then pull together all the information into an appropriate itinerary, matching the users preference for seat preferences, frequent-flyer club and dietary requirements. Once the itinerary was prepared, an *automation agent* would go back out on to the Internet to make the reservations and would return the appropriate confirmations to the user (Dombey, 1998b).

## 5.7 A Word of Warning

None of the technologies described throughout this text – with the possible exception of widespread interactive television – are futuristic. In most cases, they have already been successfully applied to tourism marketing and distribution throughout the world. These systems will continue to evolve and new ones will develop as the race to bring tourism information and reservations facilities to the consumer continues.

The question of whether to distribute electronically has been answered. Travel marketers no longer need to try to decide between using GDS or CRS or the Internet, because with the growing acceptance of open systems, the technology, to a large extent, does not matter anymore. In addition, no single channel is likely to become dominant in the near future and multiple, parallel channels are likely to co-exist, each appealing to different market segments. Instead, travel marketers must ensure that they are ready to take advantage of opportunities as they arise. Even though the precise mechanism by which data are transmitted or communicated will change as technology develops, those suppliers who have succeeded in supplementing their existing print-based sales and promotional material with appropriate data in digital form will be capable of exploiting any emerging electronic distribution channels. The digital age is upon us and the time to act is not tomorrow but today.

# Case Study 11: The Hotel Guide

The Hotel Guide AG (THG) is a Swiss-based company that was founded in 1991 and is using new technology in a very traditional business – the publication of hotel guides. By using multiple distribution channels, they ensure that their product is used by as wide an audience as possible, thus helping to increase the sales of their member hotels.

THG's database is very comprehensive both in terms of the number of hotels listed (over 60,000) and in terms of the amount of information stored about each property. While many hotel guides cover highly frequented locations such as New York, Paris and London, THG also features a comprehensive range of less well known destinations on all six continents. Each hotel listing includes the hotel's size, price level, facilities and contact information to make a reservation. Each is graded as to its level of luxury using a five-star rating. In addition, many listings include colour photographs and detailed descriptions, together with links to the hotel's Web site (Fig. 5.A).

The database is aimed at both the individual traveller and the travel trade, and it can be accessed in a number of ways. A printed version is produced annually, mainly for use by travel agents. A CD-ROM-based version is also available, which is updated twice annually and the database can also be accessed over the World Wide Web (www.hotelguide.com). This gives visitors free access to the database, is updated monthly and is reputed to be one of the largest international hotel directories on the Web. Advertisers pay a single fee to be included in all three media. Distributing the data in three ways helps THG to utilize their investment in developing and maintaining the database. However using the database in one of its electronic formats is more convenient for the customer, as it allows them to take advantage of powerful search facilities to find appropriate hotels based on geographical location, price range or facilities, as can be seen from Fig. 5.B.

The Web site currently receives over 200,000 visitors per month. It facilitates the booking process using a printed form. This is generated by entering the dates and types of rooms required into a Web form, which is then reformatted into a single printed page containing all the relevant details (including the hotel's fax number, any special

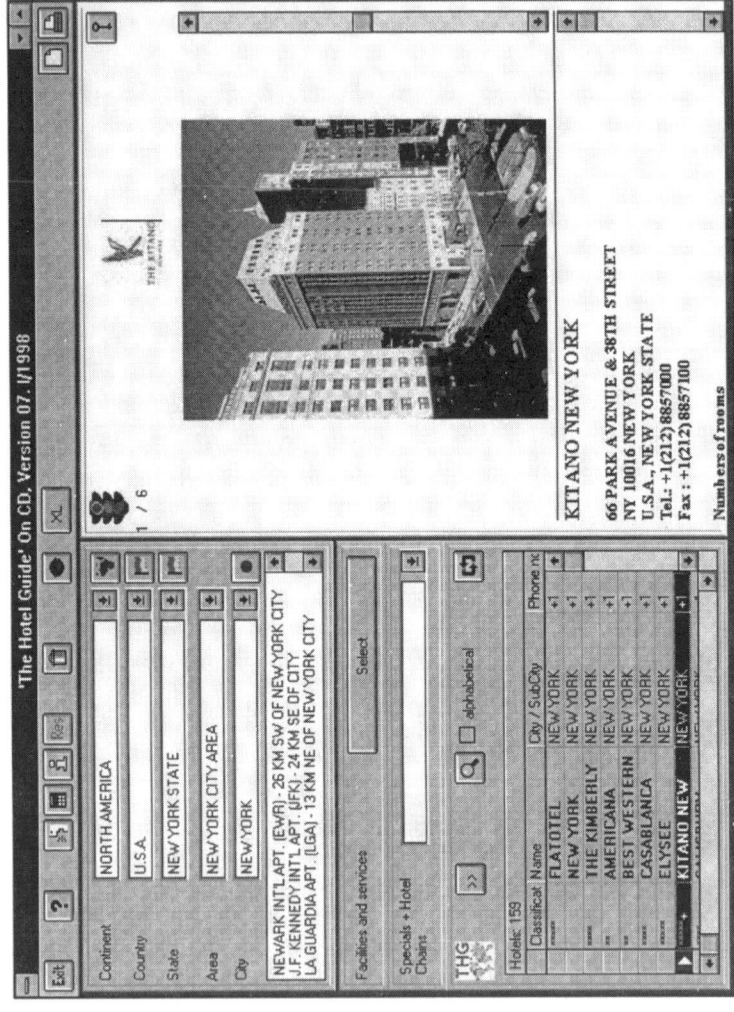

**Fig. 5.A.** Sample screen from THG's CD-ROM product.

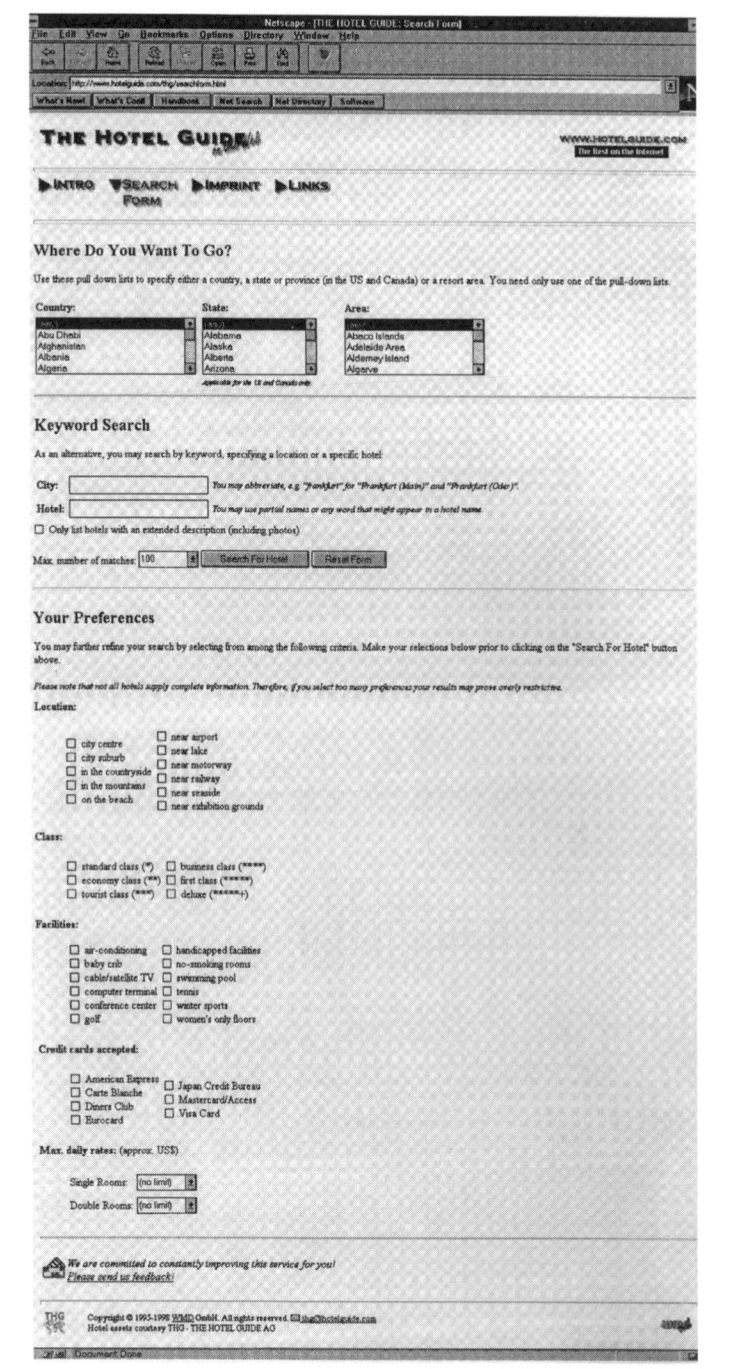

**Fig. 5.B.** The THG Web search form.

requests and the payment method to be used). The user then has to print this and fax it to the hotel to make the reservation. The fax sheet also contains instructions for the hotel reservations department, telling them that the enquiry originated from THG and telling them to reply directly to the customer. Email is also possible (again with the reservation details being added automatically), and in both of these cases, no commission is payable as the booking comes directly from the client. Future developments to the site will include more multimedia content, and online booking facilities, as well as improved statistical feedback to advertisers on the effectiveness of their pages.

# Case Study 12: The Imminus Travel and Tourism Intranet

## Introduction

During the late 1970s and early 1980s, the automated sale of package holidays was introduced in Europe on a large scale with the implementation of national videotext-based reservation systems, such as START in Germany and Istel, Prestel and Imminus' Fastrak in Britain. The three British videotext networks are also referred to as *Viewdata*. Each of these communication platforms is based on the use of keyboard and terminal to enter and display information, using private (and public) communication networks to transmit information to and from central computers. Although simple in technological terms, at the time of its introduction it represented a significant leap forward in operational terms for the package travel sector. By 1987, 85% of all package holiday bookings were being made through Viewdata, and it is estimated that there were 23,000 terminals distributed among the UK travel agency network. However, Viewdata suffers from a variety of limitations, including poor quality operational speed and very basic graphics capability. Despite both this and the emergence of new technologies such as the Internet and multimedia, today Viewdata still remains the main platform for the distribution of holiday packages in Britain.

Increasingly, however, tour operators, travel agents and other travel and tourism organizations in Britain perceive the need to replace Viewdata with a new platform. Obviously, there is a reluctance to discard the major investment in Viewdata technologies, and there is also little consensus among the industry as to which new technologies to adopt. Imminus is proposing a migration from Viewdata to a new technology platform, referred to as a travel and tourism intranet/extranet. In essence, the proposed solution allows for the co-existence of Viewdata and new, mainly Internet-based technologies, thereby enabling travel and tourism companies to continue using their present and proven systems, while at the same time giving them the opportunity to cost-effectively adopt new technologies. The proposed system is designed to provide the benefits of the Internet, and its associated technologies, within an environment that can support the very specific business processes and practices of the travel and tourism industry. It has been piloted during September and October 1997, with the first live booking having been made on 15 October 1997 between the travel agent Apollo Travel and the tour operator Crystal Holidays. A limited roll-out was taking place during early and mid 1998, with a full roll-out planned for the following months.

### Imminus/General Telecom Limited

Imminus was founded by The Thomas Cook Group as Travinet Limited in the early 1980s, based on an internal IT division. After a take-over of Thomas Cook by the Midland Bank PLC in 1983, Travinet was renamed Midland Network Services (MNS). The Midland Bank itself was acquired by the Hong Kong Shanghai Bank in the early 1990s. While Thomas Cook was sold to WestLB in June 1992, MNS was taken over in a management buyout in July 1993. In March 1994, the company was renamed Imminus (Latin, essentially meaning 'imminent'). General Cable PLC (one of the largest companies in the United Kingdom) acquired Imminus Ltd in March 1997, and integrated the company into the newly formed General Telecom Ltd (GTL), which focuses on the business-to-business communications market. GTL owns and manages extensive X.25, Frame-Relay and high-speed ATM (asynchronous transfer mode) data networks as well as voice networks in the UK. The 'Imminus' name was retained as a brand for the Travel Division as the company controlled an estimated 50% of the online holiday reservations market in Britain. In late 1996, a strategic business decision was taken by the senior management at Imminus to develop and implement the Imminus Travel and Tourism Intranet to capitalize on the company's position and take advantage of developing technologies.

### System Operation

Browsers are loaded on travel agent PCs and workstations to allow access to the Intranet service. (The option of a thin-client approach also exists, with all software including Web browsers operating in the network.) The interface consists of a number of data entry screens (effectively Web pages), which allow the user to enter appropriate details to book holidays or access holiday services (Fig. 5.C). The system is specifically designed to make the travel agent's job less boring and repetitive. For example, multiple, simultaneous enquiries can be made using one set of entry screens, and the system can be configured to search on preferred suppliers' systems automatically.

As the system is based on Web browsers, high-quality graphics,

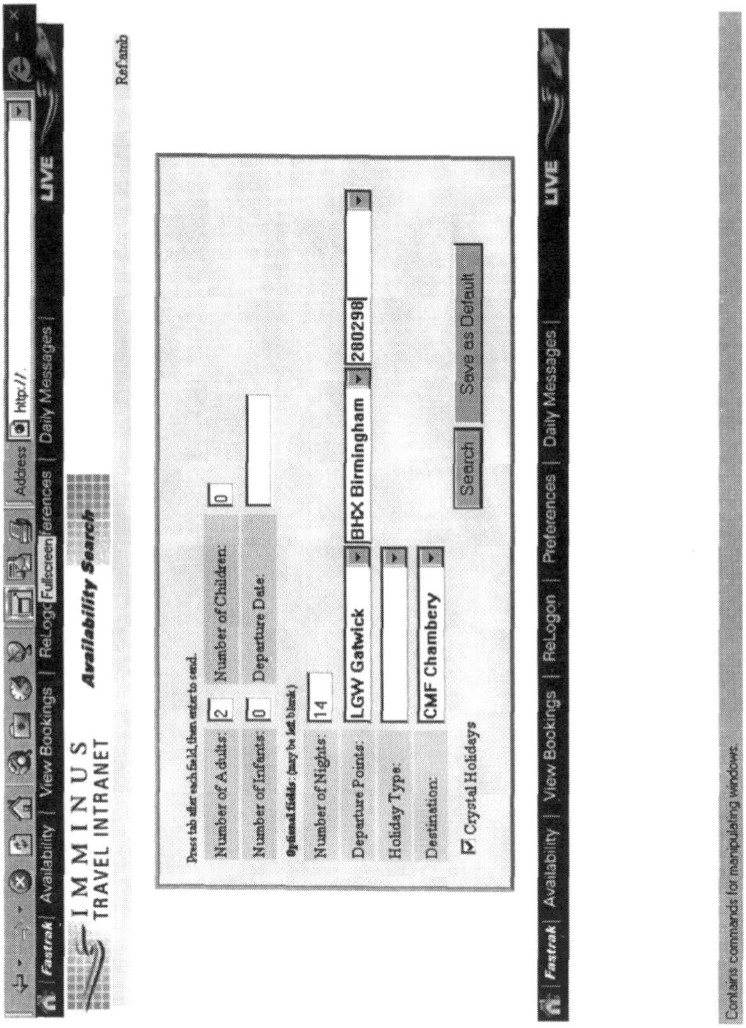

Fig. 5.C. The Imminus Intranet search screen.

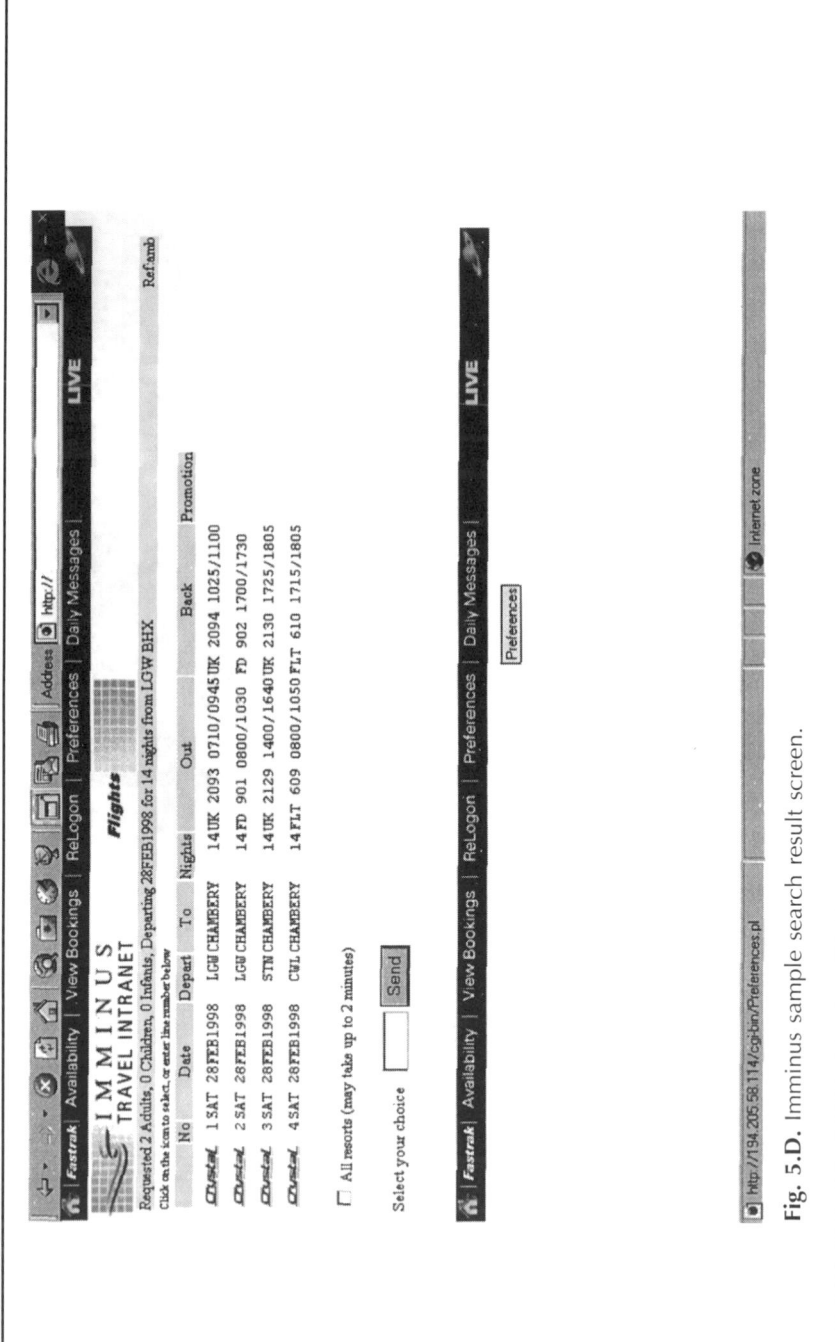

**Fig. 5.D.** Imminus sample search result screen.

images, video clips and audio clips can also be displayed on the travel agents screen, thus helping to sell the product more effectively. These facilities, however, can be configured by the travel agent to ensure that they are only used where they are beneficial. For instance, it may not be appropriate to show online images of resorts or hotels to support the sale of a 'bucket-and-spade' holiday as this would slow down the sales process. However, for higher margin products, such as cruises or safaris, the provision of such extra information and pictures may mean the difference between a sale and a no-sale, or may lead to the sale of 'travel-extras' at premium prices. Information flow between the Intranet and the tour operator reservation systems is handled by an EDI (electronic data interchange) module.

Structured messages generated by the reservation system are received by this module and converted into hypertext mark-up language (HTML) for display on the travel agent's Web browser (Fig. 5.D). Similarly, data entered into a Web form by the agent goes through the interface and is translated into an industry standard structured message format and forwarded electronically to the tour operator reservation system. In addition, the system allows for the co-existence of Viewdata and IP (Internet protocol)-based technologies, and thus suppliers can have access to a new, low-cost distribution channel without having to throw out their investment in videotext systems.

The use of the Intranet-based system benefits both parties involved. Suppliers benefit from a new, powerful channel of distribution, with standard technologies, predictable transaction costs and low capital requirements. In addition, they have the opportunity to migrate to newer technology and thus provide better service to their travel agent customers. Travel agents benefit from an improved user interface, leading to less frustration and lower training costs and, since the system is designed to specifically match the business practices and commercial needs of agents, improvements in productivity are also possible.

There is no doubt that the tour operator sector in the UK needs to upgrade the technology that it uses for package holiday distribution. The question is when and how will it happen? The Imminus Travel and Tourism Intranet offers the industry a clear route forward that minimizes the risks, problems and costs associated with change. If the initial stage of the project is accepted by the industry, it will allow Imminus to develop and market a set of additional Intranet services. These will focus on enhancing the functionality of the system, by, for example, providing a travel picture library containing images of hotels and tourist attractions that can be used in brochures or displayed on travel agent screens. The system could also manage a generic late-availability database that would provide travel agents with

a single source of late-availability holidays while also allowing suppliers to off-load their unsold inventory at the last minute. Other services that could be incorporated include online interactive training
and new information services targeted at specific segments of the
industry. The incorporation of such facilities would turn the Intranet
into a total information service for travel agents, but obviously its economic feasibility is first of all dependent on it becoming the primary
transaction processing system for package holiday bookings in the UK.

# References

Anon. (1968) Reservation systems – communication networks that sell rooms. *Cornell Hotel and Restaurant Administration Quarterly*, 11–16 February.

Anon. (1993) A CRS service for the independents. *Hospitality and Automation Report* 3 (2), 8.

Archdale, G. (1993) Computer reservation systems and public tourist offices. *Tourism Management*, 3–14 February.

Archdale, G., Stanton, R. and Jones, C. (1992) *Destination Databases – Issues and Priorities*. Pacific Asia Travel Association, San Francisco.

Arthur Andersen (1998) *The Future of Travel Distribution – Securing Loyalty in an Effective Travel Market*. Arthur Andersen, New York.

Baker, M., Hayzelden, C. and Sussmann, S. (1996) Can destination management systems provide competitive advantage? A discussion of the factors affecting the survival and success of destination management systems. *Progress In Tourism and Hospitality Research* 2, 1–13.

Bathory-Kitsz, D. (1996) Inventing the internet presence. *RIS News*, June/July, pp. 8–14.

Bender, D. (1995) The Internet – using the World Wide Web to market tourism. *HSMAI Marketing Review*, Fall, pp. 8–14.

Bender, D. (1997a) Using the Web to market the hospitality, travel and tourism product or service. *HSMAI Marketing Review*, Fall, pp. 33–39.

Bender, D. (1997b) *Marketing on the Web – Internet Strategies For Hospitality, Travel and Tourism*. Hospitality Sales and Marketing Association, Washington, DC.

Bennett, M. (1993) Information technology and travel agency – a customer service perspective. *Tourism Management*, August, pp. 259–266.

Bennett, M. (1996) Information technology and databases for tourism. In: Seaton, A. and Bennett, M. (eds) *The Marketing of Tourism Products: Concepts, Issues and Cases*. Thomson International Business Press, London, p. 423.

Bennett, R. (1998) 'The booking process: the developers perspective', Presentation at EuroHotec, Nice. International Hotel and Restaurant Association, Paris.

Bloch, M. (1996) An open letter to travel agents – survival tips for the electronic era. *Business Travel News*, 9 September, no. 354.

Bloch, M. and Segev A. (1997) The impact of electronic commerce on the travel industry – an analysis methodology and case study. In: *Proceedings of the 30th Hawaii International Conference on System Sciences (HICSS)*, Hawaii.

Bloch, M., Pigneur Y. and Segev A. (1996a) On the road of electronic commerce – a business value framework, gaining competitive advantage and some research issues. In: *Proceedings of the 9th International EDI-IOS Conference*, Bled, Slovenia.

Bloch, M., Pigneur Y. and Steiner T. (1996b) The IT enabled extended enterprise: applications in the tourism industry. In: Schertler, W., Schmid, B., Tjoa, A.M. and Werthner, H. (eds) *Information and Communication Technologies in Tourism (ENTER). Proceedings of the 3rd International Conference*. Innsbruck, Austria. Springer-Verlag Wien, New York.

Bordat, P. (1995) *Tourism and Information Technology*. World Tourism Organization, Madrid.

Breakwell, S. (1997) The Internet Travel Opportunity. Presentation at the World Travel Mart, Berlin.

Buhalis, D. (1996) Enhancing the competitiveness of small and medium-sized tourism enterprises. *EM – Electronic Markets* 6 (1), 1–6.

Buhalis, D. (1997) Information technology as a strategic tool for economic, social, cultural and environmental benefits enhancement of tourism at destination regions. *Progress in Tourism and Hospitality Research* 3, 71–93.

Buhalis, D. (1998) Strategic use of information technologies in the tourism industry. *Tourism Management* 19 (5), 409–421.

Buhalis, D. and Cooper, C. (1992) Strategic management and marketing issues for SMTEs: a case study of the Greek Aegean Islands. In: Teare, R., Adams, D. and Messenger, S. (eds) *Projects in Hospitality Organizations*. Cassell, London, pp. 101–125.

Buhalis, D. and Main, H. (1996) Information technology in small/independent Welsh and Aegean hotels. In: *Proceedings of the Hospitality Information Technology Association Conference*, Edinburgh. HITA, London.

Burns, J. (1995a) Electronic GDS distribution – what are your options. *Hospitality and Automation Report* 3 (5), pp. 1, 3, 11.

Burns, J. (1995b) Seamless – the new GDS connectivity standard. *Hospitality and Automation Report* 3 (5), pp. 5, 9.

Burns, J. (1995/96) Hospitality marketing through Global Distribution Systems. *HSMAI Marketing Review* 11 (4), 12–17.

Burns, J. (1996) A landmark year for hotel CRS. *Hospitality and Automation Report* 4 (2), pp. 4, 15

Burns, J. (1998) CRS – evolving roles, evolving capabilities. *Lodging*, June, pp. 79, 81.

Cahill, J. (1995) Internet – a link for business. In: *The Communication Superhighway: From Multimedia to Personalized Service*. UFTAA–IHA Automation Seminar, International Hotel Association, Paris.

Cahill, J. (1996) Internet, the power, problems and potential. *The Bottomline*, June/July, pp. 18–21.

Castleberry, J., Hempell, C. and Kaufman G. (1998) *Electronic Shelf Space on the Global Distribution Network*. Hospitality and Leisure Executive Report, Arthur Andersen, New York.

Cho, W., Connolly, D. and Tse, E. (1995) Cyberspace hospitality: is the industry ready? *Hospitality and Tourism Educator* 7 (4), 37–40.

Christensen, E. (1998) The booking process: the developers' perspective. Presentation to EuroHotec, 26/02/98. In: International Hotel and Restaurant Association (1998) *Eurhotec Conference Report*, International Hotel and Restaurant Association, Paris.

Coby, A. (1993) Bringing in the business. *Caterer and Hotelkeeper*, 25 March, 52–53.

Connell, S. (1996) TIM and SAM – use of technology to create new business relationships for tourism. *EM – Electronic Markets* 6 (1), 12–14.

Copeland, D. (1991) So you want to build the next SABRE system? *Business Quarterly* 55 (3), 56–60.

Coyne, R. (1995) The reservations revolution. *Hotel and Motel Management*, 24 July, 54–57.

Coyne, R. and Burns J. (1996) Global connectivity. *Hotel and Motel Management*, 22 April, 28–29.

Crichton, E. and Edgar, D. (1995) Managing complexity for competitive advantage – an IT perspective. *International Journal of Contemporary Hospitality Management* 7 (2/3), 12–18.

Davis, S. and Davidson, B. (1991) *2020 Vision: Transform Your Business Today to Succeed In Tomorrow's Economy*. Simon and Schuster, New York.

Deighton, J. (1996) The future of interactive marketing. *Harvard Business Review*, November–December, pp. 151–162.

Dombey, A. (1998a) Hotel and destination distribution on GDS and CRS. Presentation at IT Action 2000, Northampton, May. English Tourist Board, London.

Dombey, A. (1998b) Separating the emotion from the fact – the effects of new intermediaries on electronic travel distribution. In: Buhalis, D., Tjoa, M. and Jafari, J. (eds) *Information and Communication Technologies in Tourism (ENTER). Proceedings of the 5th International Conference, Istanbul, Turkey*. Springer-Verlag Wien, New York.

Dorren, K. and Slater, A. (1996) Leveraging tourism information onto the Web. In: *Proceedings of the Hospitality Information Technology Association Conference*, Edinburgh. HITA, London.

Edwards, G., Dawes, C. and Karcher, K. (1998) The Imminus travel and tourism Intranet. Presentation at the 5th International Conference on Information and Communication Technologies in Tourism – (ENTER), Istanbul, Turkey. Springer-Verlag Wien, New York.

Emmer, R. and Tauck, C. (1993) *The Hotelier's GDS Education Manual*. HEDNA and School of Hotel Administration, Cornell University, HEDNA, Pittsburg.

Emmer, R., Tauck, C. and Moore, R. (1993) Marketing hotels using Global Distribution systems. *Cornell Hotel and Restaurant Administration Quarterly*, December, pp. 80–89.

Ernst, Matthias and Walpuski, Dirk (1994) Information technologies and tourism markets. In: Schertler, W., Schmid, B., Tjoa, A.M. and Werthner, H. (eds) *Information and Communication Technologies in Tourism (ENTER). Proceedings of the 1st International Conference, Innsbruck, Austria*. Springer-Verlag Wien, New York.

European Commission (1993) *Microeconomic Analysis of the Tourism Sector.* European Commission, DGXXIII, Brussels.

Financial Times Service (1998) *Barclays Introduce Service with Links to Retailers.* 3 April 1998.

Francese, P. and Renaghan, L. (1990) Database marketing – building customer profiles. *Cornell Hotel and Restaurant Administration Quarterly,* May, pp. 60–63.

French, H. (1994) Destination management systems – Canadian experience in the development of destination management systems. In: Jordan, Y. (ed.) *Information for Travel and Tourism Marketing: a Tool for Profit. Proceedings of the Pacific Asia Travel Association Conference.* Pacific Asia Travel Association, Vancouver, British Columbia.

French, T. (1998) The future of Gobal Distribution Systems. *Travel and Tourism Analyst* 3, 1–17.

Frew, A. and O'Connor, P. (1998) A comparative examination of the implementation of destination marketing system strategies: Scotland and Ireland. In: Buhalis, D., Tjoa, M. and Jafari, J. (eds) *Information and Communication Technologies in Tourism (ENTER). Proceedings of the 5th International Conference, Istanbul, Turkey.* Springer-Verlag Wien, New York.

Frew, A. and O'Connor, P. (1999) Destination marketing system strategies: refining and extending an assessment framework. In: Buhalis, D., Tjoa, M. and Jafari, J. (eds) *Information and Communication Technologies in Tourism (ENTER). Proceedings of the 6th International Conference, Innsbruck, Austria.* Springer-Verlag Wien, New York (in press).

Frew, A. and Pringle, S. (1995) Multi-media marketing across ATM Broadband networks – a hospitality and tourism perspective, Part One. In: *Proceedings of the Hospitality Information Technology Association Conference, New Orleans.* HITA, London.

Gilbert, D., Powell Perry, J. and Widijoso, S. (1998) A study of the hotel industry's application of the Internet as a relationship marketing tool. In: *Proceedings of the 3rd International Conference on Tourism and Hotel Industry in Indo-China and Southeast Asia: Development, Marketing and Sustainability, Phuket, Thailand.* Pacific Asia Travel Association, San Francisco.

Gilbert, R. (1996) Reservation sales – point of sales or cost of sales. *HSMAI Marketing Review* 13 (2), 37–41.

Ginsburg, L. (1997) Doing business on the Web. *Windows Magazine,* April, pp. 207–216.

Go, F. and Pine, R. (1995) *Globalization Strategy in the Hotel Industry.* Routledge, New York.

Haines, P. (1993) *Destination Databases: the Pacific Asia Travel Association Perspective.* Occasional Paper Series, PATA, San Francisco.

Haines, P. (1994) Destination marketing systems. In: Schertler, W., Schmid, B., Tjoa, A.M. and Werthner, H. (eds) *Information and Communication Technologies in Tourism (ENTER). Proceedings of the 1st International Conference, Innsbruck, Austria.* Springer-Verlag Wien, New York.

HEDNA (1997) *GDS Trends Survey.* HEDNA, Pittsburg.

HEDNA (1998a) *Travel Distribution Report,* 5 (20), 15 January. HEDNA, Pittsburg.

HEDNA (1998b) *Onward Distribution of Hotel Information via the Global Distribution Systems.* HEDNA White Paper, HEDNA, Pittsburg.

HEDNA (1998c) Annual GDS net reservations statistics. Press release, April 1998.

Heintzeman, S. (1994) Marketing through technology. *Hotel Management International* 2, 127–129.

Hitchins, F. (1991) The influence of technology on UK travel agents. *EIU Travel and Tourism Analyst* 3, 88–105.

Hoffman, D. and Novak, T. (1996) Marketing in hypermedia computer-mediated environments: conceptual foundations. *Journal of Marketing* 60, 50–68.

HSMAI (1995) Get on the Internet or else. *Hospitality (UK)*, April/May, p. 10.

HSSS (1994) Central reservations for the small group. *HSSS Newsletter* 4 (5), 6–7.

HSSS (1995) Forte reformed. *HSSS Newsletter* 5 (4), 4–5.

Huddart, G. (1998) The global view. *Travel News and Perspectives*, June, pp. 158–159.

Hurst, S. (1992) Industry presentation – accommodation and attractions perspective. In: Yee, J. (ed.) *Proceedings from the PATA Destination Database Conference, Singapore, December 9–10.* PATA, San Francisco.

Hyung-Soo, J. and Baker, M. (1998) Assessing the market effectiveness of the World Wide Web in national tourism offices. In: Buhalis, D., Tjoa, M. and Jafari, J. (eds) *Information and Communication Technologies in Tourism (ENTER). Proceedings of the 5th International Conference, Istanbul, Turkey.* Springer-Verlag Wien, New York.

IMRG (Interactive Media In Retail Group) (1996) *Building, Managing and Prospering With Commercial Web Sites.* IMRG, London.

Inkpen, G. (1994) *Information Technology for Travel and Tourism.* Pitman Publishing, London.

Inkpen, G. (1998) *Information Technology for Travel and Tourism*, 2nd edn. Pitman Publishing, London.

Jennings, M. (1996) Wired for a new era. *Airline Business*, August, pp. 22–23.

Jones, C. (1992) Destination databases as keys to effective marketing. In: Yee, J. (ed.) *Proceedings from the PATA Destination Database Conference, Singapore, December 9–10.* PATA Intelligence Center, San Francisco.

Jones, C. (1993) *Applications of Database Marketing in the Tourism Industry.* PATA Occasional Paper Series, PATA, San Francisco.

Jupiter Communications (1997) *Travel and Interactive Technology: a Five Year Outlook.* Jupiter Communications, New York.

Karcher, K. (1996a) *Reinventing the Package Holiday Business.* Deutscher Universitats Verlag, Weisbaden.

Karcher, K. (1996b) The four global distribution systems in the travel and tourism industry. *EM – Electronic Markets* 6 (2), 20–24.

Kasavana, M. and Cahill, J. (1992) *Managing Computers in the Hospitality Industry*, 2nd edn. Educational Institute of the American Hotel and Motel Association, East Lansing, Michigan.

Kaven, W. (1974) Channels of distribution in the hotel industry. In: Rothmell, J. (ed.) *Marketing in the Services Sector.* Winthrop Publications, Cambridge, Massachusetts, pp. 114–121.

Kingsley, I. and Fesenmaier, D. (1995) Travel information kiosks: an emerging communications channel for the tourism industry. *Journal of Travel and Tourism Marketing* 4 (1), 57–70.

Klein, S. and Langenohl, T.J. (1994) Co-ordination mechanisms and systems architectures in electronic market systems. In: Schertler, W., Schmid, B., Tjoa, A.M. and Werthner, H. (eds) *Information and Communication Technologies in Tourism, Proceedings of the 1st International Conference, Innsbruck, Austria.* Springer-Verlag Wien, New York.

Knodt, D. (1997) The future of the travel agent. Presentation at the 4th International Conference on Information and Communication Technologies in Tourism – (ENTER), Edinburgh. Springer-Verlag Wien, New York.

Knowles, T. and Garland, M. (1994) The strategic importance of CRSs in the airline industry. *EIU Travel and Tourism Analyst* 4, 4–6.

Kotler, P. (1984) *Marketing Management: Analysis, Planning and Control.* Prentice Hall, Englewood Cliffs, New Jersey.

KPMG (1998) *Europe Gets Wired – a Survey of Internet Use In Great Britain, France and Germany.* KPMG, London.

Main, H. and O'Connor, P. (1998) The use of smart card technology to develop a destination-based loyalty/affinity scheme for SMEs in tourism and hospitality. In: Buhalis, D., Tjoa, M. and Jafari, J. (eds) *Information and Communication Technologies in Tourism (ENTER). Proceedings of the 5th International Conference, Istanbul, Turkey.* Springer-Verlag Wien, New York.

Manente, M., Minghetti, V. and Mangilli, V. (1998) The electronic management of business travel: an integrated approach. In: Buhalis, D., Tjoa, M. and Jafari, J. (eds) *Information and Communication Technologies in Tourism (ENTER). Proceedings of the 5th International Conference, Istanbul, Turkey.* Springer-Verlag Wien, New York.

McGuffie, J. (1994) CRS development in the hotel sector. *EIU Travel and Tourism Analyst* 2, 53–68.

Meijer, E. (1995) Practical use of Compuserve and Internet for the travel and hotel industry. In: *The Communication Superhighway: From Multimedia to Personalized Service.* UFTAA–IHA Automation Seminar, International Hotel Association, Paris.

Middleton, V. (1994) Special characteristics of travel and tourism. In: Middleton, V. (ed.) *Marketing in Travel and Tourism.* Butterworth Heinemann, Oxford.

Milchem, H. (1997) Destination reservation systems – can they meet the challenge? In: Tjoa, M. (ed.) *Information and Communication Technologies in Tourism (ENTER). Proceedings of the 4th International Conference, Edinburgh.* Springer-Verlag Wien, New York.

Moran, N. (1997) Business to business links: now the attention turns to Extranets. *Financial Times* 4 June, 5–6.

Murphy, J., Forrest, E. and Wotring, C. (1996a) Restaurant marketing on the World Wide Web. *Cornell Hotel and Restaurant Administration Quarterly*, February, pp. 61–71.

Murphy, J., Forrest, E., Wotring, C. and Brymer, R. (1996b) Hotel Management and Marketing on the Internet. *Cornell Hotel and Restaurant Administration Quarterly*, June, pp. 70–82.

Mutch, A. (1996) The English Tourist Network Automation project: a case study in interorganizational system failure. *Tourism Management* 17 (8), 603–609.

Naisbitt, J. (1994) *The Global Paradox*. Avon, New York.

Odell, M. (1996) Smart cards to chip in – Europe. *Airline Business*, August, pp. 24–25.

Olsen, M. (1997) *Events Shaping the Future and their Impact on the Multinational Hotel Industry*, International Hotel and Restaurant Association, Paris.

O'Connor, P. and Frew, A. (1998) The evolution of hotel electronic distribution. In: *Proceedings of the HSMAI / EuroCHRIE Conference, Oslo, Norway*. Hotel Sales and Marketing Association International, Oslo.

Pegasus Systems (1998) Pegasus Systems to Pay Travel Agents for Internet Hotel Bookings. Press release, 20 July.

Petitt, G. (1993) CRS Tech: focus on the basics. *Lodging Hospitality*, February, p. 28.

Pollock, A. (1992) *Information Technology and the Emergence of a New Tourism*. PATA Occasional Paper Series, PATA, San Francisco.

Pollock, A. (1995a) The Impact of Information Technology on Destination Marketing. *EIU Travel and Tourism Analyst* 3, 66–83.

Pollock, A. (1995b) *The Role of Electronic Brochures in Selling Travel: Implications for Businesses and Destinations*. PATA Occasional Paper Series, PATA, San Francisco.

Pollock, A. (1997a) Building an intelligent destination management system (IDMS©) – an overview of technical aspects. Presentation at the 4th International Conference on Information and Communication Technologies in Tourism – (ENTER), Edinburgh.

Pollock, A. (1997b) Creating intelligent destinations for wired consumers: a conceptual framework and its Scottish application. Presentation at the 4th International Conference on Information and Communication Technologies in Tourism – (ENTER), Edinburgh.

Pollock, A. (1997c) Marketing destinations on the Internet – why and how? Presentation at the 4th International Conference on Information and Communication Technologies in Tourism – (ENTER), Edinburgh.

Pollock, A. (1997d) *Destinations as Networked Enterprises*. The Pembridge Group, Stratford-upon-Avon.

Poon, A. (1989) Competitive strategies for a new tourism. In: Cooper, C. (ed.) *Progress in Tourism, Recreation and Hospitality Management*. Belhaven Press, London, pp. 91–102.

Poon, A. (1988) Tourism and Information Technologies. *Annals of Tourism Research* 15, 531–549.

Poon, A. (1993) *Tourism, Technology and Competitive Advantage*. CAB International, Wallingford, UK.

Poon, A. (1994) The new tourism revolution. *Tourism Management* 15 (2), 91–92.

Pringle, S. (1995) Computer reservation systems: their strategic and operational implications for the UK hotel industry. PhD thesis, Napier University, Edinburgh.

Puetz-Willems, M. (1996) Spanning the globe. *European Hotelier* 1, 22–23.

Pusateri, M. and Manno, J. (1998) Travelers take to the 'Net. *Lodging*, June, pp. 23–24.

Reinders, J. and Baker, M. (1998) The future for direct retailing of travel and tourism products: the influence of information technology. *Progress in Hospitality and Tourism Research* 4, 1–15

Richards, G. (1995) Retailing travel products: bridging the information gap. *Progress in Tourism and Hospitality Research* 1, 17–29.

Richards, L. (1992) Europe – is it that different? *Hospitality and Automation Report* 2 (1), 4–5.

Roache, G. (1997) In bed with the Internet: buying or just browsing? In: *Proceedings of the Australian Tourism and Hospitality Research Conference*, p. 568.

Rowe, M. (1995) Sailing on the Internet. *Lodging Hospitality* 38, 43–44.

Schaeffer, B. (1994) Using technology to reach the travel trade. In: *Information For Travel and Tourism Marketing – a Tool For Profit, Proceedings of the PATA Conference, Vancouver, BC*. PATA, San Francisco.

Schmid, B. (1994) Electronic markets in tourism. *The Tourism Review* 2, 9–15.

Schonland, A. and Williams, P. (1996) Using the Internet for travel and tourism survey research: experience from the net traveller survey. *Journal of Travel Research*, Autumn, 81–87.

Schulz, A. (1996) The role of global computer reservation systems in the travel industry today and in the future. *EM – Electronic Markets* 6 (2), 17–20.

Selwitz, R. (1993) THISCO turns on hotels with improved system. *Hotel and Motel Management* 1 November, 61, 66.

Sheldon, P. (1993a) Destination information systems. *Annals of Tourism Research* 20, 633–649.

Sheldon, P. (1993b) *Issues in the Development of Destination Information Systems*. PATA Issues in Tourism Series, no. 1, San Francisco.

Sheldon, P. (1995) *Global Distribution Systems Update 1995*. PATA, San Francisco.

Sheldon, P. (1997) *Tourism Information Technology*. CAB International, Wallingford, UK.

Steiner, T. and Dufour, A. (1998) Agent based cybermarketing in the tourism industry. In: Buhalis, D., Tjoa, M. and Jafari, J. (eds) *Information and Communication Technologies in Tourism (ENTER) Proceedings of the 5th International Conference, Istanbul, Turkey*. Springer-Verlag Wien, New York.

Sussmann, S. and Baker, M. (1996) Responding to the electronic marketplace: lessons from destination management systems. *International Journal of Hospitality Management* 15 (2), 99–112.

Sykes, L. (1998) Power traveler. *The Sunday Times*, 26 April, s 5, 6.

Teare, R. (1993) Designing a Contemporary Hotel Service Culture. *International Journal of Service Industry Management* 4(2), 63–73.

Tellini, A. (1995) Models of Hotel Promotion on the WWW, http://gwis.circ.gwu.edu/~iits/journal/modelwww.htm

Travel Industry Association of America (1998a) Online Travel Revenue Triples in 1997 (press release), http://www.tia.org/press/021098jupiter.stm

Travel Industry Association of America (1998b) Travel Agencies Still Preferred Source for Travel Information (press release), http://www.tia.org/research/summinternet97.asp

Troy, T. (1993) Hotel chains integrate systems to bolster profits. *Hotel and Motel Management* November 1, 60, 62, 64, 67.

UFTAA–IHA (1995) *The Communication Superhighway; from Multimedia to Personalised Service.* Seminar Proceedings, 17th UFTAA and 5th IHA Joint Seminar for Travel Agents and Hoteliers, International Hotel Association, Paris.

Vallauri, D. (1995) GDS connectivity altering travel business. *Lodging Hospitality*, October, p. 51.

Vellas, F. (1997) Les reseaux informatises et le transport aerien. In: *Le Tourism: une Dynamique de Reseau.* ERTSEC, Le Mirail, 5, University de Toulouse.

Vlitos-Rowe, I. (1992) Destination databases and management systems. *EIU Travel and Tourism Analyst* 5, 84–109.

Vlitos-Rowe, I. (1995) *The Impact of Technology on the Travel Industry – Developments and Trends.* Financial Times Management Reports, London.

Wagner, G. (1991) Lodging's lifeblood. *Hospitality*, December, p. 105.

Walle, A. (1996) Tourism and the Internet: opportunities for direct marketing. *Journal of Travel Research*, Summer, pp. 72–77.

Wardell, D. (1998) The impact of electronic distribution on travel agents. *Travel and Tourism Analyst* 2, 5–6.

Welch, S. (1995) Room bookings via global distribution systems: the European dimension. In: *Proceedings of The Hospitality Information Technology Association Conference, New Orleans.* HITA, London.

Werthner, H. (1997) The relationship between information technology and tourism. *Tourism and Technology Bulletin* 2, pp. 14–15.

Wingfield, N. (1998) Up in the air – digital TV is coming. *Wall Street Journal Europe*, 19 March, 10.

Wolff, C. (1996a) Tapping into the travel bazaar. *Lodging Hospitality* 52 (3), 43.

Wolff, C. (1996b) Maturing of a critical appliance. *Lodging Hospitality* 52(9), 60.

WTO (1991) *Tourism to the Year 2000 – Qualitative Aspects Affecting Global Growth.* World Tourism Organization, Madrid.

WTO (1995) *Global Distribution Systems (GDSs) in the Tourism Industry.* World Tourism Organization, Madrid.

WTO (1997a) Faced with Worldwide Competition and Structural Changes, What are the Tourism Responsibilities of European Governments? WTO / CEU-ETC Joint Seminar, Salzburg, Austria.

WTO (1997b) Hotel industry think tank reveals extent of Internet revolution. *Tourism and Technology Bulletin* 2, 9.

# Index